EX LIBRIS

GROUND COVER

GROUND COVER

A THOUSAND BEAUTIFUL PLANTS FOR DIFFICULT PLACES

John Cushnie

KYLE CATHIE LIMITED

To Laura Baura, who has a love of all books – with love from Dad

To Bob Flowerdew, who germinated the seed; Caroline Taggart who kept the plant growing; and my wife Wilma, whose encouragement and help ensured that it bloomed – thank you.

JOHN CUSHNIE

First published in Great Britain in 1999 by
Kyle Cathie Limited
122 Arlington Road
London NW1 7HP

Reprinted 2000

ISBN 1 85626 326 6

A CIP catalogue record for this book is available from the British Library.

Half-title Contrasting leaf shapes make a striking display.
Title spread (left) Sedum spectabile takes centre stage in a border of colour; *(right)* A mass planting of ornamental cabbages 'Lyssako' at the Château de Villandry in France.
This page Polygala calcarea 'Lillet'.
Overleaf Hosta, Cynara and *Cistus* dominate a lush border in a city garden.

Project editor Caroline Taggart
Designed by Prue Bucknall
Edited by Sue Hook
Printed by Kyodo Printing Co Pte Ltd, Singapore

CONTENTS

AN INTRODUCTION TO
GROUND COVER

■ **Above** Ornamental kale
variety 'Coral Queen' in the
dead of winter. You have
only to drive through any
commercial vegetable-growing
region to realize how good
some types of brassicas are as
ground coverers. Large
evergreen leaves, low-growing
and planted closely for
maximum crop, are ideal for
excluding weeds. Good
autumn and winter color is a
useful bonus.

■ **Opposite** An attractive
mixed planting of ground
covering, with the added
advantage of eye-catching
spring color.

WHAT IS GROUND COVER?

In putting pen to paper (to me a word-processor is a television with no picture) to address the subject of ground-cover plants I realize that to some gardeners such plants are no more than a means to weed control. Although many plants can be used for this purpose, there are other useful applications for coverers.

Areas that are difficult to manage – such as steep banks where weeds and soil erosion are a problem or grass terraces where the cutting of grass is tedious – can benefit from a planting of labor-saving ground cover. Excessively wet or dry sites that are difficult to cultivate may be covered with well-chosen plants and kept beautiful with the minimum of follow-up maintenance. Banks of streams, shaded woodland and light-starved beds at the base of north-facing (in the northern hemisphere) walls all are candidates for ground-cover plants.

There is an enormous range of plant material that will cover the soil, some more obvious than others. Perhaps this book will encourage you to choose from heathers, conifers, herbaceous plants, alpines, herbs, shrubs, ferns, grasses, climbers and even fruit and vegetables. The curriculum vitae of most suitable plants will mention that the applicant requires little or no maintenance. If you have to give a ground-cover plant more than its share of man hours you might as well save your money and spend the time weeding.

The plants selected for ground cover by most landscapers and designers are by nature low-growing, rampant, spreading, creepy-crawly things and yet successful ground cover requires no such thing. To my mind, the ideal description of a ground-cover plant should include, 'bold, dense mass of leaves completely covering the ground most of the year; evergreens gain brownie points'. The leaves don't have to be immediately above the soil, but if they prevent light and moisture penetrating to the soil surface you are well on your way to reducing weeds. For example, I would argue that a bold planting of hybrid rhododendron, camellia or aucuba makes superb ground cover. For weed suppression, plants don't need to 'stoop to conquer'.

KISS

A fundamental way of ensuring that your garden actually works is to adopt the KISS principle (Keep It Simple, Stupid). Nature is a good teacher, choosing plants that are best suited to the local conditions. The chalky English South Downs play host to dogwood, guelder rose, spindle and boxwood with no visiting rhododendron in sight. Acid heathland welcomes birch, pine, gorse, bracken, heathers and rhododendron and they all live together happily.

In our gardens we often seem to thrive on impossible projects and between 'keeping up with the Joneses' and showing off the rarest, most expensive or newest plant on the market we continue to place unsuitable plants in situations guaranteed to ensure their death or a miserable life of torture. You and your plants will be much happier if you choose those that suit your site. Having said that, I am not opposed to changing what nature has provided since in most modern homes the site is 'made up' (usually badly). Prior to building good topsoil is often scraped off and sold to last year's new gardeners who are trying to improve their lot. The subsoil is churned up and compacted by machinery, with lashings of rubble, timber offcuts and broken slates thrown in. The surface is then levelled and a sprinkling of topsoil added like icing sugar on Turkish Delight. In no way can such a mutilated medium provide a healthy start for your plants.

Get to know your plot – dry or wet, sunny or shaded, acid or alkaline, windy or sheltered, heavy soil, rich soil or poor, hungry soil. These are the criteria that help you determine your choice of plant. But don't despair – even if you have wet, shaded, acid, windy, heavy soil you can grow hostas, as good a plant as you could wish for. Later I will list plants for special situations and between you and me we will think of something for every site.

■ Bold, leafy and evergreen, rhododendrons will form a dense canopy, preventing weeds from growing underneath.

FIND OUT ABOUT YOUR SOIL

Most plants have preferences for particular soil conditions. If you don't know whether your soil is acid or alkaline, you cannot hope to choose ground cover (or any other) plants that are ideally suited to your unique site. The acidity or alkalinity of soil is measured in terms of pH. Without boring you with a lot of detail, pH is a logarithmic scale which ranges from zero to fourteen. Soils with a pH over 7.0 are alkaline or limy, those with a pH below 7.0 are termed acidic. The further away from 7.0 you get, the more extreme the acidity or alkalinity is. Most soils fall between 5 and 9. There are lots of simple test kits on the market that will give an accurate pH reading but it is important to take three or four soil samples from different areas of the garden. A single sample could give an inaccurate reading because one area of soil may differ from another, especially in a large garden.

Very few plants enjoy boggy soil. It is cold and inhospitable, preventing the rapid growth so desirable for ground-cover plants. A moist, open-textured, easily warmed soil is ideal, but you can do a lot to improve conditions that fall short of perfection.

When faced with waterlogged or badly drained soil the first step is to identify the cause. Poor drainage may be due to compacted soil, a high water table or excessive run-off from surrounding land. Quite often it is caused by surface compaction of the soil, which prevents water filtering through. Breaking the crust of the soil often solves the

problem. Add grit, compost, well-rotted farmyard manure or spent mushroom compost to open up the soil and enrich it with humus, which most plants appreciate.

If this does not help – and particularly if the soil is heavy clay – you will probably require proper pipe and stone drains. Unless you are confident about digging these yourself, seek the advice of an experienced groundwork contractor.

With the exception of trees, most plants are interested in the topmost 8–10 in (20–25 cm) of soil and if this is in good condition and loose enough to plant you can ignore what is below. However, if you decide to accept your site for what it is, you can still find plants that are adapted to awkward conditions. For example, permanently water-logged soil allows the planting of shallow-rooting, or marginal, plants that enjoy having their feet in water. Equally, a thin topsoil with underlying rock close to the surface will indicate a choice of plants that can tolerate drought conditions.

■ *Hosta fortunei* 'Aurea Marginata' is an ideal ground-covering plant, tolerating a wide range of soil types and climatic conditions.

■ **Opposite** Growing
potatoes is a good way of
reducing the weed population.
The dense leaf cover will
suppress even strong-
growing weeds and you
can eat the crop.

SOIL PREPARATION

The trouble is that many of our best-known ground coverers can become weeds and the description 'grows like a weed' is firmly rooted in truth and common sense. A good definition of a weed is a plant that isn't wanted in its particular location. I have nightmares of gardeners in Nevada and New Mexico hoeing out cactus plants and nurturing dandelions, picking their attractive blooms for buttonholes.

There are three types of weed that cause trouble. Perennial weeds are the worst and can be subdivided into those that spread by seed and those that increase by root or stolon. Then there are annual weeds that grow from seed, last only one season but multiply quickly and spread widely in a short time. The third type that can cause trouble to gardeners are the trees and shrubs that also seed or sucker and can become weeds in themselves. Ash, sycamore, cotoneaster, hebe and stag's horn sumach are all guilty.

Beware the 'friends' who give you a bucketful of 'pieces' surplus to their requirements. They will almost certainly be plants that have outgrown their welcome and that their owners are glad to see the back of. Deadnettle (*Lamium*) and creeping Jenny (*Lysimachia*) are only worthwhile if ruthlessly restricted to their allocated plot and not allowed to colonize the garden. Cut back the extension growth each autumn, digging out any rooted pieces that are spreading too far. Dump the prunings on the compost heap. Why is it that only mint comes with the health warning 'grow in a plunged bucket'?

Most gardeners think of good ground cover not as short-term planting but rather as permanent, soft landscaping that will serve a useful purpose for many years. As such you are only going to get one chance to prepare the ground, so try to get it right first time. Don't take short cuts or the plants may not live to regret it.

There are two vital steps to take before rushing in with your newly acquired plants. Before you begin any planting program it is imperative to remove all perennial weeds. On a small scale even the most invasive and deep-rooted weeds can be eliminated by digging or forking to remove every last piece of root. On a large scale some form of chemical weed control is probably necessary and glyphosate-based products are the safest and most reliable to use. The chemical is sprayed on actively growing leaves in midsummer and is translocated to the root, where it kills from the bottom up. Persistent weeds such as docks and nettles will require repeated applications. Glyphosate is deactivated when it comes in contact with the soil so can be described as a 'green' weed control. I will discuss chemical weed control in more detail on page 24.

Choose a windless day for chemical spraying and be especially careful to avoid spraying close to plants. Spray drift may cause loss of leaf, distortion or even death of the plant. It is also possible to kill weeds by spreading black polythene or old carpet over the soil surface. If this is left in place for eighteen months, even strong perennial weeds will die off for lack of the light which is necessary for photosynthesis – the chemical process by which plants manufacture food – to take place. Please, if you must use carpet, lay it upside down, to avoid a jigsaw of colors and the admission that your previous carpet was cheap.

Annual weeds are usually fairly easily cleared but the trick is to eliminate them before they form seed. Since most of them have a shallow root structure they can be pulled by hand or hoed off. Leaving the root is not a problem but if plants are removed

before they flower and seed there will be fewer next time around. Unfortunately some annuals produce about four crops each year, so at no time can you afford to lower your guard. Every time the soil is turned over and opened up a new batch of weeds will germinate, so if time permits it is sensible to hoe or fork over the newly weeded patch and then leave it for a few weeks to allow another crop of weeds to germinate and be removed before planting.

When you are sure that the site is weed-free, cultivate thoroughly by digging and raking to produce a fine, stone-free tilth ready for planting. Incorporate compost and bone meal, which are slow-release organic fertilizers. Bone meal produces nitrogen and phosphate for up to nine months.

If you have the time and the skill I would recommend hand-digging the area for planting. I mention skill, not with a view to artistry but rather to prevent back pain. Hundreds of years ago, it seems, I was taught to dig properly by Fred Power, the demonstrator at Greenmount College in County Antrim, where I studied, and to this day I can dig for hours without serious mishap. You shouldn't have to bend your back to dig, so choose a spade with a shaft the right length to suit your height. Keep your back straight and turn the blade full of soil over using your wrists rather than twisting at the waist.

Hand-digging with a good-quality, wooden-shafted spade, turning the soil upside down the full depth of the blade, is the best way to get to know your soil and its content. Earthworms, or the lack of, will be noticed and pests such as leather jackets identified and eliminated. Bits of weed roots can be removed and if a surface dressing of compost has been applied this can be turned in about 8 in (20 cm) deep. In cold periods the soil can be left rough to allow the frost to penetrate. This will break up heavy soil and kill overwintering pests. If you're lucky enough to live in a frost-free garden, just rake the soil to a fine tilth after digging.

Rotivating is a very impersonal and crude way of preparing soil. Many of the smaller machines only have the power to stir up the top few centimeters or inches, chopping perennial weed roots up into smaller pieces and creating perfect conditions for new weeds to multiply.

If you have purchased plants but are not certain that your site is thoroughly weed-free it is best to wait. Young plants can be temporarily housed in a nursery bed or potted up and nurtured until the ground is clean and the weather is suitable for planting.

When planting dig a hole larger than the pot or root area of the plant. A good handful of bone meal in the base of the planting hole and some compost or old farmyard manure worked in around the roots will get the plant off to a good start. Plant at the same depth as the plant was previously growing – you will see the soil ring around the main stem – and firm well to remove any air pockets, using your knuckles around small plants and your feet for larger plants. Water the root area well after planting, even if it is raining (though you don't half feel daft if people see you standing in the rain watering plants). The water will help settle the soil around the roots and reduce the risk of the plant withering.

■ **Opposite** These municipal gardens in Barcelos, Portugal feature a mass planting of *Ajuga reptans* forming a carpet edged with box hedging.

When ground cover is in the form of carpeting plants such as ajuga you will find that a quicker and more total cover is achieved by putting lots of small, carefully divided pieces of plant fairly closely together. Larger, well-spaced clumps will take longer to join together and the spaces between them will tempt new weeds to germinate. Where possible tease the clumps of plants apart, taking care not to tear the roots but separating into individual, rooted pieces. Plant as soon as possible after dividing to prevent the plants drying out.

Larger shrubs should be spaced so that they do not overlap and lose their natural shape when they mature. If they are too close together they will have to compete for food, water, sunlight and air, and if enough is not available they become stunted. Properly spaced they should meet and form a continuous spread of foliage after a few seasons. In the meantime weeds will try to grow in the gaps, but hoeing or mulching will keep them at bay until you have light-excluding leaf cover. If cost allows, plant the spaces with quick-growing carpeters such as *Cotoneaster* 'Skogholm' and *Vinca major* to smother any emergent weed seedlings. These will in turn be smothered by the permanent, taller plants.

PLANTING WITH WEEDS IN MIND

The three ways to achieve quick total ground cover are to plant closely, to plant quick-spreading plants and to feed the plants to encourage growth.

When close planting it is best to use only one type of carpeting plant. If you mix more than one species it is almost inevitable that one will be stronger growing than the other and will choke it.

Speedy coverers are fine if they have lots of space or if you can control them, but some are so rampant as to become weeds in their own right. The winter heliotrope (*Petasites fragrans*) and mints such as the Corsican mint (*Mentha requienii*) spread rapidly, not stopping to read the Trespassers Will Be Prosecuted signs. Nitrogen feeds will guarantee quick growth, but if applied regularly they produce weak plants, giving poor cover and subject to frost damage.

One solution is to plant closely and then thin the plants before they grow into one another. Transplant the surplus into gaps or use them to extend the overall planting.

Plants that spread, rooting as they grow, will enjoy a loose surface tilth or a mulch that encourages rooting, such as old mushroom compost or leaf mould. During the first year annual weeds will sprout in uncovered patches of soil, but are easily controlled by cultivation with a hoe or a rake on a loose soil. Some plants such as rhododendron, camellia, box and philadelphus have very shallow surface roots; it is not advisable to hoe around these as some of the roots will be severed, putting the plant under even more pressure during dry weather.

There is little point in hoeing during wet weather as weeds are often left lying on the surface with the roots intact. They will soon reroot and perform even better than before as transplanted seedlings with less competition. All seedling weeds should be raked off and dumped or composted.

■ **Above** Lush green shuttlecock fronds contrasting with English bluebells.

■ **Left** *Euphorbiu urnygdaloides robbiae* is happy to share a bed with naturalizing *Scilla bithynica*.

CHOOSING PLANTS

The choice of ground-cover plants for your garden will depend on your site: location, size, exposure and soil conditions. You have to make personal decisions about the height and spread of plants, their flower and fruit color, perfume, whether or not you want evergreens and the level of maintenance you are willing to put in.

One other big decision has to be made. Will the area be planted *en masse* using a large number of the same plant, giving uniformity of height and color? Will it be a mixture of different plants with different leaf shape and flowering period but still growing to about the same height? Or a mixture of plants maturing at different heights to give a tiered, skyline effect?

I tend to support the last scheme as I enjoy a changing scene with something different to look at throughout the year. Once it comes to zimmer time I will probably wish for a more practical planting, with less pruning, dead-heading, sucker removal or thinning out to be done. Small groups of plants make more of an impression than individual ones and for years I recommended planting in odd numbers – say five or seven or eleven heathers. Then I questioned what I preached and started planting six or eight or eighty in a drift. It didn't make one bit of difference to the overall scheme, providing they were not planted in straight lines or in blocks, but I have never worked out whether it saved me a plant or cost me a plant.

It does make sense to position low-growing plants to the front, with taller plants behind. This prevents material being lost to view and possibly choked. You can, however, plant the occasional larger-growing specimen through low ground cover to create interest and give height. Select a plant that won't spread too much, as the underplanting will suffer. Island beds marooned in a sea of grass or gravel and viewed from all sides lend themselves to a planting of taller material in the center of the bed, gradually reducing in height towards the edge.

Give some consideration to color when deciding your planting scheme. Shades of green are restful; mixed foliage with variegated, blue and plum-colored leaves can be eye-catching. In this respect conifers score highly. Flower colors should be compatible and while no color is out of place in the garden some don't mix as well as others. Blue and yellow is a winning combination, providing the blue is a good solid color, not a pale wishy-washy blue or, even worse, a shade of mauve. Personal choice allows for many other color mixes. Orange and white work well together, as do red and white mixtures, providing there is a mass of white flowers and the dead blooms are picked off before they turn brown. White on its own is difficult, and a border of different white flowers can be a nightmare, because no two whites are exactly the same and the result is often an unattractive near miss. Cerise and yellow plants flowering together remind me of an inferior pizza.

■ **Opposite** Living proof that ground cover doesn't have to be made up of low-growing, creepy-crawly green plants.

■ **Top** Excellent for ground cover in shady areas, *Lamium galeobdolon* spreads rapidly, rooting as it goes.

■ **Above** *Pachysandra terminalis* forms a dense evergreen mat in full or partial shade, but dislikes growing in dry soil.

Planting under existing evergreen trees is a headache. The mass of roots compete for every inch of space, the nutrients have long since been exhausted, the topsoil is probably devoid of moisture, light levels are low and rain will drip in large drops damaging leaf and flower. Beneath conifers the soil may even be poisoned by toxic needle droppings, and rhododendrons can poison the soil, preventing other plants from growing. In situations like these your choice is limited, but Irish ivy or pachysandra are two that will give a good account of themselves.

ACQUIRING PLANTS

One of the most popular ways of obtaining plants is through the generosity of your friends. However, the plants offered are usually thinnings of invasive plants that they would like to be rid of. So be it; if you have a large area to cover, invasive plants are just what you need. Later you can be fussy. Don't plant those with long tap roots: they will be difficult to control and to uproot if they spread too far. Lamium, ajuga, vinca and pachysandra are all vigorous spreaders, but provided they are ruthlessly restricted to their plot they are excellent ground-coverers. If I ever discover a new variety of lamium I will call it meek, because the good book says that the meek shall inherit the earth.

Local nurseries are great treasure troves for plants, but unfortunately retail nurseries are becoming thin on the ground. They are closing down to be sold to developers or turned into trade-only outlets or garden centers. The big advantage of a nursery is that if the plants are grown locally they are more likely to succeed in your garden than if they have been brought in from elsewhere. Generally speaking at a nursery you will also get good down-to-earth advice thrown in for free.

Mail order can be very satisfactory provided the company has a good reputation and you remember to make allowance for sales tax and postage and packing costs. It is advisable to check what size of plant is offered as most mail order companies specialize in young and therefore small plants that are easily packed and dispatched. Damage during delivery is rare, as modern packaging and speedy despatch ensure that plants arrive well-protected and fresh.

Garden centers are the accepted source of plants and all that you need by way of sundries. By shopping around you may well find significant differences in the prices of plants. This may be attributed to variations in plant quality or the power of bulk purchasing, lower mark-up percentages or simply a good value sale.

When purchasing check that the plants are container grown and not just recently containerized. To do this, try removing the pot. If the roots aren't visible or the compost is loose and liable to fall off, don't buy the plant. The root system should be capable of holding the compost as a root ball. A containerized plant will suffer a check in growth if the compost falls away, exposing bare roots when the plant is removed from the pot.

The other problem may be a plant that has been in the pot for more than a season and is pot-bound with the roots packed tightly together. Weeds or moss growing in the top layer of compost is one indication of this. It is essential that these roots are teased out before planting, to allow them to spread into the surrounding soil.

■ **Opposite** *Vinca minor* 'Argenteomarginata', the small-leafed variegated periwinkle, will suppress annual weeds and enjoys a woodland situation.

Always be wary of plants whose compost is dry. Peat-based and soil-less composts, and even some composts using peat substitutes such as coir are very difficult to wet thoroughly once they have dried out, and if planted out with a dry root-ball no amount of watering will penetrate to the roots. Plunge dry root-balls in a bucket of water and leave them submerged for a few hours to allow the compost to soak through before planting.

WEED CONTROL

I have emphasized that for success with ground cover it is essential that all perennial and strong-growing weeds are eliminated before planting. From hard-won experience I can appreciate that, even with your best endeavors, this may not be possible. Even pro-fessionally executed ground-cover landscape planting schemes can go wrong and when they do it is frequently because of weeds. By its very nature ground-cover planting inhibits the removal of weeds as much as it prevents weeds growing. It is only right that this section should look in detail at the problem of and solutions to weeds.

There are two stages to a weed-free planted area: get it clean and keep it clean (by clean, I mean clean of weeds). The theory is that if you clear the ground of weeds, if you choose the right mix of plants and if they cover the ground quickly you will have no weed problem. A lot of ifs, but the theory frequently works perfectly in practice, so let's start to 'get it clean'.

Winter is a bad time to judge the weed population in a new garden. A lot of the worst culprits will have died down, leaving little evidence on the surface. Horsetail, ground elder, bindweed, nettle and willow herb are all passive during prolonged cold periods, appearing again to cause havoc at the onset of warm weather. If you can adopt the attitude that another six months won't make much difference to the growth of new plants, then wait until vigorous growth starts before you do your weeding.

Perennial docks, dandelion and thistle send long tap roots straight down like carrots but twice as far. Bindweed (*Convolvulus*) has pure white or pale brown roots that will extend horizontally for long distances, covering 3–6 feet (1–2 m) in a season. Miss a piece ½ in (1 cm) long and it will grow away with a vengeance. If you are conscientious and diligent you stand a good chance of getting all the weeds. Be aware that often the source of perennial weeds is your neighbor's garden or an old boundary hedge where it is impossible to cultivate or apply weedkiller. Weeds seem to know that they have protection in these 'safe areas' and will continue to grow out in all directions without fear. The best remedy for illegal immigrants is to dig a trench about 20 in (50 cm) deep along the boundary, line both back and sides with thick polythene and back-fill with soil.

Perennials that spread by seed are more difficult to control in that they are spread by wind, water, bird droppings or the movement of soil. In theory, if you prevent your dandelions from flowering their numbers won't increase; in practice your neighbor's seeds will drop in by parachute.

Trees and shrubs can be a ready source of seedlings, most of which are unwanted. If removed at seedling stage they are unresisting, but once they get established it is a digging job. It never ceases to amaze me the way a sycamore sapling gets missed until

■ Opposite Color combinations can be the making of a planting scheme. Although color is very much a matter of personal taste, strong contrasts such as this juxtaposition of rosemary and cytisus are much more pleasing to my eye than wishy-washy mixtures of pastel shades.

it is about 18 in (45cm) high. Cutting them back to ground level simply allows them to regenerate and produce three times as many stems.

If you have reached this stage and have done your best, you can do no more, so plant with confidence.

CHEMICAL WEED CONTROL

The lobby for reduced use of herbicides or weedkillers is stronger than ever before and who can blame them? Undoubtedly, chemicals that we thought were safe and used extensively have now been taken off the market because there is some degree (however slight) of risk to the health of the soil, animals or humans. Most of the trouble has been caused by commercial use by landowners, farmers and landscape contractors who found that herbicides were the only way to control weeds on a large scale. The quantities used by gardeners were significantly less but nevertheless added to the overall build-up.

Having said that, I still believe in chemical weed control. Used properly it is an extremely useful method of weed prevention and elimination. Instead of saying, 'Use no chemicals', I think that it would be much more sensible if we said, 'The chemicals we use must be 100 per cent safe.' This is not impossible, it simply needs extensive research, and that means lots of money. There are already simple, soap-based products that break down to fatty acids and yet are capable of killing weeds. Let's have more of these. Weedkillers used to be divided into contact, residual, translocated (systemic) and total, but a lot of the residual weedkillers and the total types that contained residuals are no longer available. The most popular brands now on the market are based on contact or translocated chemicals. Residuals remained in the soil (and also leached into waterways) and prevented weed seeds growing after germination. Contact chemicals simply kill the leaves that come into contact with the weedkiller and are used mainly on soft annual weeds and grasses. Translocated herbicides are perhaps the most useful in eradicating perennial weeds. The chemical enters the leaf and is carried through the plant to the roots, which it kills. It is much more effective than those that simply burn the leaf off leaving the root to grow again. Dock and giant hogweed, for example, throw up fresh green shoots almost immediately after being sprayed with a contact weedkiller. Total weedkillers were exactly that, killing everything, lasting for a considerable period and mainly used for patios, paths and drives.

The trouble with most herbicides for plant use is that, unlike lawn weedkillers, they are not selective. In turf you can kill a whole range of weeds without harming the grass. Not so with ornamental plants, and for low-growing ground cover they are of limited use. Prior to planting, herbicides can be used to clear the site and subsequently to spot-treat between plants. When the day comes that I can spray selectively for weeds over the top of my plants with a product that is as safe as all the other chemically based items that we use, such as toothpaste, perfume, soap and hand cream, I will be a very happy gardener and probably very, very old.

FERTILIZERS, ADDITIVES AND MULCHES

Like you and me, plants can suffer as much from overfeeding as from underfeeding. Too many gardeners apply fertilizer to the plants in the same way as I was given cod-liver oil as a child – 'Get it down you it will do you good.' I wonder if it ever did do me good.

Moderation is the key. Most plants need feeding only once or twice a year and then only in the growing season, when they can put the nutrients to good use. When rapid, leafy growth is required, a high nitrogen feed is the answer, but the resulting growth will be soft and easily damaged by cold winds and frost. Spreading plants will enjoy extra feeding until they have filled their allocated space. But don't overdo it. Bugle, for example, will respond to nitrogen by producing green leaves without any of the bronze and yellow dappling that is so attractive. The flowers will also be scarce when otherwise the plant would be

■ Mulching with bark chips will deter weeds and help retain moisture, forming a fine peat-like layer as it rots down.

smothered in blue. The other two main nutrients are phosphate and potash, but they are more useful for producing steady growth, with strong roots and good flower color, than for rapid growth.

If you want to treat your plants and get a favorable reaction, apply an annual organic mulch, 4–6 in (10–15 cm) deep, to all but the compact ground huggers. Mulching keeps the soil warm, helps retain moisture and suppresses weeds. Old seed or potting compost, spent growbag compost, home-made compost or leaf mould are all fine enough to wash down through the leaves to form a layer at soil level, encouraging the plant to develop new roots and rejuvenate itself. A mulch of bark or wood chippings is also attractive and useful for helping to keep down weeds, but a couple of words of caution: never top up dry or very cold soil with a deep mulch as the covering will simply shed rather than retain rain water, keeping the surface soil beneath bone dry and unable to warm up. Apply in mild weather to well-moistened, frost-free soil. A good mulch will prevent heavy soil from cracking in dry summer conditions. But as the mulch deteriorates and is broken down, helpful nitrogen bacteria are used up. So additional, high-nitrogen feeding will be required each spring to keep the nutrient balance in the soil. Lots of plants, especially native wildflowers, are quite happy in their misery and really don't enjoy feeding. Many of the alpines, for example, are content in a poor, gritty soil as long as it has good drainage. I can also think of some really dwarf cotoneasters such as *Cotoneaster congestus* that will plaster themselves with red berries if left to their own devices and yet if dosed with nutrients will be shy of fruiting.

A mulch is basically a top dressing applied to the surface of the soil, usually consisting of a bulky organic material such as old farmyard manure. Any product that keeps down weeds is to be welcomed but there are some so-called mulches that won't get my vote. If, after all, the sole purpose is to keep weeds down and to pot with the aesthetics, then lay concrete 6 in (15 cm) deep.

Lawn cuttings must be the worst mulch ever, used as an excuse for failing to dump them elsewhere. If you lay too thick a layer – more than 4 in (10 cm) – it turns into slimy muck, which is useless, and dries out to a pale, insipid, brown scab so light in weight that any self-respecting weed will push it up as it grows. If you compost mowings in a heap they have to be used in thin layers 4 in (10 cm) deep mixed with more bulky material such as autumn leaves, weeds or kitchen refuse. If the grass has been chemically treated for weed control you can't make use of the contaminated cuttings for weeks. I'm not even in favor of letting them be used as a lawn mulch except at the first and last cuts of the season. If not removed from the lawn surface during the growing season they quickly build up a layer of thatch at soil level encouraging disease and choking the grass. Large lawns will produce enormous quantities of grass cuttings and you will soon run out of space to make compost. The surplus should be bagged and taken to your recycling center.

Fresh mushroom compost is sometimes used immediately the mushroom crop has been picked, but I find that its straw content is too fresh and in spring birds scratch it out over paths and plants. It also contains significant amounts of lime, so should not be added to alkaline soil. However, if stockpiled for three or four months the same product forms a beautiful peaty-brown compost with a lot of the lime leached out and it is then ideal as a moisture-retaining surface mulch.

Bark mulch is a lovely product and is usually available in three grades. The finest is ideal for working down into the crown of plants with woody stems that won't rot, such as heathers, but has limited value as a weed deterrent. The medium grade applied about 3 in (7–8 cm) deep works a treat, looks the part and will last for at least two years. The very coarse shredded bark is more suitable to prevent injury in play or sports area, but can be used around plantings of large rhododendrons or other bulky shrubs. Wood chips are often available and sometimes wrongly labelled as bark mulch. They are the by-product of tree surgery where branches are often chipped on site, to reduce the expense and labor of taking them away. The bulk of the product is wood rather than bark and as such takes on an ashy gray appearance as it dries out. It can last a long time on the surface but uses up a lot of valuable nitrogen as it deteriorates.

Home-made products can be very useful both to save money and to recycle products that would have to be dumped or burnt. Well-shredded prunings applied as a deep mulch do the job if they are not too woody. Leaf mould is easily collected in autumn and of benefit to the plants, but it needs to be applied every year. A good compost heap can provide lots of mulching material although, unless you have a factory system producing enormous quantities of compost that can be spread at least 2 in (5 cm) deep, I would recommend digging it into the ground, where it will do most good, at planting time to provide humus. Be very careful that home-made compost is free of weed seeds as you will otherwise tend to defeat the purpose.

There is no sure-fire way of preventing weed seeds from blowing in and germinating on top of the mulch, but at least they will be sappy in their growth and easily uprooted if tackled when young, before they root through to the soil.

MAINTENANCE AND PRUNING

One of the joys of ground cover is that if the bed is well planted with suitably chosen plants, subsequent maintenance will be reduced to a minimum. Until you achieve full leaf cover you can expect some annual weeds and (surprisingly enough, considering the trouble you went to digging out every last weed) even a small number of deep-rooted, perennial weeds. Annual weeds can be scraped off and left to wither in dry weather, but deeper-rooted perennials must be eased out with a hand or digging fork. Gaps may persist through poor growth, plant deaths or over-generous spacing and every effort should be made to fill these before they are invaded by weeds. Some low-growing plants such as periwinkle, bugle and mint will root wherever the stem touches the soil; others such as strawberries will produce rooted plantlets. These can be cut away from the parent plant, lifted and replanted to fill gaps.

Apply granular fertilizer in dry weather each spring and water in well. Granular fertilizer is preferable to powdered chemicals as it is less likely to stick to wet leaves and turn into a concentrated acid which scorches the young growth. Scatter the granules so that they rattle and bounce off the foliage. If you are applying a mulch, first wet the soil well to seal in the moisture.

■ **Opposite** Michaelmas
daisies such as this *Aster novi-belgii* 'Harrison's Blue', are easily
propagated by an 'Irishman's
cutting' – snipping off rooted
shoots or stems.

Pruning promotes growth and can therefore maximize leaf cover. A pruned branch will usually generate two or three side shoots; by pruning these in turn you can quickly build up a dense framework of overlapping branches. If you cut just above a side bud the new shoot will grow in that direction. An outward-pointing bud will produce outward growth. In this way you can encourage the plant to grow evenly, covering all of its allocated space. Some plants such as hebe and cistus tend to become 'leggy' and need a hard pruning every few years to encourage new growth from the base.

Shrubs such as dogwood (*Cornus*) which are noted for their winter bark coloring should be pruned to within 6 in (15 cm) of the ground every spring to encourage the best color from new shoots. All prunings should be raked up and burnt or shredded for mulch.

PESTS AND DISEASES

Slug and snail attacks on ground-cover planting never seem as serious as on individual plants. Perhaps it is the scale of the planting. Slug damage on one hosta plant is most annoying, but a few chewed leaves on a whole patch of hostas seem hardly worth noting (until you have only a few leaves left untouched).

Keeping the area clear of rubbish and debris and a night-time patrol with a torch to collect them will help to keep snails and slugs under control. If there is a lot of debris or if the site is close to an old wall try spreading a layer of coarse grit or sharp sand around your plants (slugs and snails don't like crawling over it on their bare tummies). It seems an awful waste but beer can also be used to trap these pests. They love it and a container-full (small, mind you) at ground level will capture and drown them. What a way to go! Sour milk, orange peel and bird seed also suit their taste. Slug pellets can be used but take care to ensure that the paralysed bodies are removed promptly as the poison can be transferred to birds, hedgehogs and other small animals, including domestic pets. The pellets can also be washed away by the heavy rain beloved of snails and slugs.

Vine weevil larvae are a real pest, eating the roots of alpines and perennials and causing them suddenly to wither and die. The small, dirty-white, legless grub has a brown head and is usually found curled up. The adult beetle emerges at night to eat irregular notches from the margins of leaves, especially those of rhododendrons and hydrangeas. Control is difficult but you can try watering on one of the pathogenic nematodes availabe from garden centers. Please check the sell-by date, as these nematodes have a short life. Nematodes are a sort of thread worm, and there are tens of thousands of them in each pack. When watered into the soil or potting compost in late summer using a watering can, they will attack the vine weevil, killing the grubs before they can cause serious damage to the roots. However, this treatment won't give satisfactory results on heavy soil or soil that is colder than 14°C (57°F).

Cats can sometimes test your love. They like to use areas of loose soil as a toilet and if that results in your newly planted material being scratched out, well too bad – I like cats, but if the problem is serious hosing the surface of the soil regularly with water to keep it wet will discourage the habit. Moles are bad news. They can cause enormous damage, especially to plant roots. Do you know that we have no moles in

Ireland? So perhaps you need a leprechaun! If the situation is bad the only answer is a professional extermination service. Botrytis and gray mould may attack plants in humid weather, causing leaves, stems and flowers to rot. The best control is to remove and burn infected material and to spray regularly (i.e. once a fortnight) with a systemic fungicide.

When under stress, individual plants may suffer from all sorts of ailments, from aphids to virus attacks. A sick plant is easiest to deal with if symptoms of nutrient deficiency, disease or pest attack are noticed early. Prevention is better than cure, however, and your best insurance policy is to provide as healthy a growing environment as possible.

PROPAGATION

Quite often large quantities of plants are needed for effective ground cover and propagation serves a dual purpose, saving you a lot of money and providing the satisfaction of producing your own plants.

Producing plants from seed is a cheap way of obtaining lots of planting material but it can be slow. Seed can be sown in the soil where the plants are to grow, or germinated in compost in seed trays and transplanted as seedlings. Young plants are especially vulnerable to slugs and snails, so deter these by spreading prickly or sharp material around the plants, or be prepared to do your night patrol.

Softwood cuttings taken in early to mid-summer are easily rooted using a hormone rooting aid in liquid or powder form. The rooting compost should be a free-draining, half-and-half peat and grit medium. Trim the non-flowering cutting with a sharp knife immediately below a leaf or a pair of leaves and remove the lower leaves. The smaller the cutting the easier it is to root – 2 in (5 cm) is ideal, though fuchsia cuttings root best when less than 1 in (2 cm) long and hydrangea cuttings can be longer if the leaves are well separated. (Large leaves of hydrangea can be cut in half to reduce the transpiration which causes the cutting to wilt and die before it can root.) Insert the cuttings about 2 in (5 cm) around the edge of the pot, water in and cover with a clean, transparent, polythene bag held in place with a rubber band to reduce transpiration.

Division of herbaceous plants is another speedy way to build up a stock of plants. Clumps of perennials can be dug up during dormancy, in winter or in early spring, and carefully divided into small rooted pieces. The roots should be teased out or, in the case of large clumps, cut cleanly through with a sharp spade and replanted to form established plants quickly. It is essential that only healthy plants are divided. The older center portion of the clump should be dumped and diseased plants should be discarded or burnt as the disease will be carried by the propagated material.

Some plants can be multiplied by suckers and runners which produce rooted plants while still attached to the parent plant. Snipping off rooted shoots or stems is sometimes called 'an Irishman's cutting'. It makes me sound sort of lazy, but it works.

Pieces of roots of some plants can be used to propagate. Most gardeners are familiar with the practice of growing roots on shoots, but it is also possible to put shoots on roots. The most straightforward example is the dandelion, from which even the smallest piece of root seems capable of growing away and producing a new plant. This is a notable 'quality' of many persistent perennial weeds, but can be put to good use. Herbaceous perennials such as dicentra, acanthus and phlox can all be increased by root cuttings. They should be taken in mid-winter, when the plant is dormant, by digging the plant up, selecting strong, healthy cuttings and replanting immediately. If only a few pieces of root are required you can dig to one side of the plant (like a rabbit), remove a root or two and replace the soil with minimum disturbance to the plant.

When preparing the roots use a sharp knife. Remove any damaged buds from thick roots and trim off the thin, wiry side shoots. Cut the roots into pieces 2 in (5 cm) long. Cut straight across the root end closest to the plant and cut the other end at an angle. It is important that the pieces of root are inserted the right way up in the compost, in other words pointed end down. Cut thin roots into 2 in (5 cm) lengths and lay them horizontally on the compost.

Use seed trays or 3 in (7 cm) pots and make up a compost of equal parts peat and sharp sand. Fill to ½ in (1 cm) from the top of the tray or pot and dampen the compost before inserting the pieces of root. Dust the roots with a fungicidal powder to reduce the risk of disease entering through the cuts. Insert the pieces of root vertically in the compost about 2 in (5 cm) apart each way. The top of the root should be just level with the surface of the compost. Cover the horizontally laid thin roots with ½ in (1 cm) of compost.

Keep your cuttings well watered but not soggy. The best position for them is on a north-facing (in the northern hemisphere) windowsill in a cool room, or in an unheated glass house or frame. In spring they will break into growth and when lots of new fibrous roots have been produced you can pot them up for transplanting into the garden later in the season.

SPECIAL SITUATIONS

■ **Above** *Paeonia mlokose-witschii* enjoys a moist but well-drained soil in full sun or partial shade.

■ **Right** *Festuca*, lavender, *Stachys* and *Eryngium* all thrive in poor soil in full sun in this drought-tolerant garden in California.

For me the challenge of gardening lies in the placing of suitable plants in a given situation. As a landscaper I find that each job brings differing conditions, but proving that there is a selection of plants that will thrive in the most inhospitable site offers real job satisfaction.

Some plants are fussy and happy only in a very narrow set of conditions, and so be it. When the time comes that you need a plant for an excessively wet, acid, peaty soil in full sun, you had better hope that *Ledum palustre* is available, since it will thrive where lots of others would fail. It is not only an unsuitable soil type that can cause problems; the amount of sun or shade a site receives, wind exposure, sea spray, maximum and minimum temperatures and annual rainfall all combine to form the conditions with which the plant has to cope.

Many plants are suitable for a diverse range of habitats, excluding extremes, and these are the plants that either love you or hate you. Innumerable gardeners fret over their inability to keep alive a plant that is thriving next door. There is seldom a single answer and this is why I sometimes describe plants as 'thriving in' or 'enjoying', 'tolerating' or 'existing in' certain situations.

In this section I have matched plants with a given set of conditions, rather than specifying or changing the conditions to suit the plant – although I see no reason why soil should not be altered to make it more favorable. Draining wet soil, adding humus to sandy soil and fertilizing where necessary are all 'tools' that gardeners can use to make soil more acceptable to a particular plant.

Mass planting of a single species such as heather can be very effective, making a bold splash of color. Maintenance is easier in that the whole block of plants is treated in the same way. Using a mixture of plants can result in variety of color and interest over a longer period, and combinations that include flowers and foliage, evergreen and deciduous plants, can be practical and rewarding for twelve months of the year.

Each special situation has its own selection of suitable plants and I have chosen my favorite for each site. The combinations are again a matter of personal choice and you can try more or less anything that takes your fancy, but remember that the plants you select have to be compatible and capable of growing together. When planting in combinations, avoid plants that differ greatly in vigor or total spread, as the weaker plants will be overrun. Select colors that look good together, such as strong blues and yellows, and remember to check that they are in flower at the same time.

SPECIAL SITUATIONS

DRY SHADE

It is not easy to get plants to grow in areas of heavy shade, but by the same token most weeds have similar difficulties, so the ground cover that does succeed has less competition. In dense shade, ivy is probably the best choice for low ground cover.

In my book (and other books as well), shaded sites that are dry are the worst possible areas for planting. Overhanging trees, with a mass of roots searching out and draining the soil of all available moisture in summer, severely limit the choice of plant.

The first and essential operation is to improve the soil to the level where it will retain a degree of moisture. If the trees are deciduous there will already be a layer of leaf mould and this should be supplemented with generous helpings of well-rotted farmyard manure or spent mushroom compost. Unless you have masses of home-made compost, save it for other garden areas.

Mechanical cultivation is neither possible nor desirable where tree roots are close to the surface. Instead hand forking is needed to incorporate the compost into the surface. Beneath deciduous trees, planting in autumn may help new plants to establish before the spring leaf cover creates dense shade. Once planting is completed you will need to water regularly until the plants become established.

Plants for dry, shady sites include Irish ivy (*Hedera hibernica*). It is equally at home covering the ground or climbing and can be a bit of a nuisance if not kept in check. Spotted laurel (*Aucuba japonica*) will survive in most situations, including heavy shade, though the variegated forms will lose some of their distinctive leaf markings if they receive poor light. Female varieties produce red berries. Many of the cotoneasters will succeed as will the Oregon grape (*Mahonia aquifolium*). Butcher's broom (*Ruscus aculeatus*) makes good ground cover, the female plants producing red berries in autumn. *Geranium macrorrhizum* is a great cranesbill for dry shaded sites, plastered with pink or white blooms in early summer and growing to only 20 in (50 cm) in height.

My old favorite, as sparring partners go, is the dead nettle (*Lamium maculatum*). It is just the job for dry shaded sites and if it is very dry and very shaded *Lamium* may do as you tell it and not try to cover the whole garden.

▼ **JOHN'S CHOICE (zones 4-9)**
Variegated ground elder (Aegopodium podagraria 'Variegatum'). I am almost ashamed to admit that I like this plant, but it is not as invasive as its big, non-variegated brother and is of a more compact nature altogether. The variegated foliage is margined and splashed creamy white. Flat umbels of creamy white flowers are produced in early summer. Remove the flower heads before they set seed to control its spread.

■ **Left** *Anemone nemorosa* tolerates drought when it is dormant in summer.

■ **Right** *Viola cornuta* 'Alba' will flower from spring through until autumn, with glorious scent thrown in for free.

PLANTS BEST FOR DRY SHADE

Climber

Hedera hibernica

Fern

Polypodium vulgare

Herb

Viola odorata

Bulbs and rhizomes

Anemone nemerosa

Convallaria majalis

Oxalis adenophylla

Herbaceous perennials

Galium odoratum

Geranium nodosum

Lamium maculatum

Pachysandra terminalis

Symphytum ibericum

Shrub

Hypericum calycinum

PLANTS TOLERANT OF DRY SHADE

Alpine

Campanula portenschlagiana

Herbaceous perennials

Doronicum austriacum

Geranium macrorrhizum

Prunella grandiflora

Saxifraga marginata

Shrubs

Aucuba japonica

Mahonia aquifolium

Rubus tricolor

Ruscus aculeatus

Vinca minor

FOR MORE DETAILS OF ALL THESE PLANTS SEE THE DIRECTORY ON PAGES 92–154

GOOD COMBINATION

Wood anemone (*Anemone nemorosa*) and horned violet (*Viola cornuta*). Both these plants are delightfully dainty and easy to grow; together they will provide flowers from late winter through to summer, growing to the same height and quite happy to mix together.

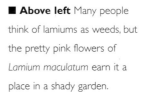

■ **Above left** Many people think of lamiums as weeds, but the pretty pink flowers of *Lamium maculatum* earn it a place in a shady garden.

■ **Left** *Viola odorata*, English violet or sweet violet, has a wonderfully sweet scent and self-seeds freely.

■ **Right** *Polypodium vulgare* 'Cornubiense' is ideal for gritty, well-drained soil.

DAMP SHADE

Moist and shady areas of the garden are easier to deal with than dry shade, provided they are not completely waterlogged. Quite often trees overhang moist boggy areas but the shade is not usually very dense. The biggest problem is that the site can change from boot-sucking mud to cracked, parched clay in a period of weeks. Digging lots of grit into the top 6 in (15 cm) will encourage drainage and reduce the risk of surface cracks.

For sites that stay damp, however, there is a wide range of suitable ground-cover plants. Hostas have to get a mention even though they die down in winter. Their large, satiny leaves are available in a range of shades from blue green to palest yellow green and every pattern of yellow and white variegation. Unfortunately slugs and snails love hostas for breakfast, dinner and tea and unless you take steps to protect the plants they will even snack between meals. However, there are two hostas that these pests seem to dislike, leaving them unscathed while others close by are ravaged. *Hosta* 'Zounds' and *H.* 'Sum and Substance' are worth trying.

The giant cowslip (*Primula florindae*) loves moist, shady conditions, flowering at over 36 in (90 cm) high and releasing an exquisite perfume. Gaultherias are happy in moist, shady sites, and will spread rapidly to give complete cover. The vincas are also content to spread through moist soil at a satisfactory rate, forming a solid carpet of green or variegated leaves with blue or white periwinkle flowers.

Then there is the distinctly unpleasant, shady and cold site at the base of a sunless wall. The soil is often mossy and sour and the introduction of some organic material from time to time will help the few plants that can survive in this situation. Just for good measure the bed will probably be damper than surrounding areas. *Ledum groenlandicum* will do, provided the soil is lime-free. *Lonicera pileata* is a semi-evergreen honeysuckle, growing to about 40 in (1m) high and tough enough for a cold wall.

■ **Left** Good late spring color with candelabra primula and *Alchemilla mollis*, ladies' mantle, in the foreground. *Phalaris arundinacea* 'Feesey', ribbon grass (back left), will grow anywhere.

■ **Above right** *Astilbe* 'Professor van der Wielen', a good reliable herbaceous plant that is guaranteed to flower every year.

■ **Right** *Asplenium scolopendrium* 'Crispum Group' hart's tongue fern, likes an alkaline soil and, unlike many ferns, is not invasive.

▼ **JOHN'S CHOICE**

Ourisia microphylla. *This little gem loves a damp, fertile soil in shade, forming a 2 in (5 cm) high cushion of dark green leaves. From late spring into summer it smothers itself with pale pink single flowers.*

PLANTS BEST FOR DAMP SHADE

Climbers

Hedera

Lonicera pileata

Fern

Asplenium scolopendrium

Bulbs, rhizomes and tubers

Arisaema sikokianum

Arisarum proboscideum

Galanthus nivalis

Ourisia microphylla

Pachysandra terminalis

Trillium grandiflorum

Herbaceous perennials

Aegopodium podagraria 'Variegata'

Ajuga reptans 'Multicolor'

Astilbe 'Professor van der Wielen'

Helleborus foetidus

Helleborus orientalis

Hosta fortunei

Shrubs

Mahonia nervosa

Prunus laurocerasus 'Otto Luyken'

Skimmia japonica

PLANTS TOLERANT OF DAMP SHADE

Herbaceous perennials

Helleborus argutifolius

Primula florindae

Shrub

Ledum groenlandicum

FOR MORE DETAILS OF ALL THESE PLANTS SEE THE DIRECTORY ON PAGES 92–154

GOOD COMBINATION

Wake robin (*Trillium grandiflorum*) and toad lily (*Tricyrtis flava*) complement each other without competing, the wake robin with its pure white flowers in spring and summer and the toad lily making its display of yellow with purple spots in autumn.

■ **Above left** *Helleborus orientalis*, the Lenten rose, flowers from mid-winter to mid-spring, providing a welcome splash of color.

■ **Left** A bright patch on the winter scene: snowdrops and variegated ivy provide a cheerful carpet in a woodland situation.

■ **Right** *Helleborus foetidus*, the stinking hellebore, has an unpleasant smell when the leaves are crushed, but the bell-shaped green flowers are usually more agreeably scented.

FULL SUN

Sites in full sun should be the easiest to plan but soil conditions play a large part in determining suitable plants and can cause problems of their own.

Soils that are not retentive of moisture are like mini-deserts and can be the death of all but the toughest of ground cover. Incorporating lots of home-made compost and moisture-retentive material such as spent mushroom compost, rotted farmyard manure or leaf mould will help the soil hold water. Thorough watering until the plants become established, and heavy surface mulches of shredded bark, leaf mould or compost will be beneficial. Mulches must be applied when the soil is moist and frost-free (i.e. in late winter) to seal in the moisture. A mulching material spread on dry soil will prevent water from penetrating the ground, thereby making the problem worse.

It is difficult to establish plants in clay soils which dry out in summer to a consistency vaguely resembling concrete and split by cracks that always seem to appear right beside the plants. Tackle this problem whenever the soil is workable by digging in lots of coarse grit, leaf mould or peat. This will separate the particles and open up the heavy soil, reducing the risk of it baking hard.

Many of the plants that enjoy full sun and can do with a minimum of water are unfortunately susceptible to even a hint of frost. This often means that they have to be treated as carpeting annuals with perhaps the bonus of overwintering safely.

The red valerian (*Centranthus ruber*) actually does best in poor, under-nourished soil and self-seeds effortlessly. *Convolvulus cneorum* loves full sun, but should be protected from cold wet winters. *Cistus* and the lavenders thrive in dry, sun-baked, light soils, but also dislike cold wet winters, so are best planted with a gravel top-dressing to help drainage and with some shelter from cold winds. *Ceanothus* likes dry conditions and with the nickname of Californian lilac, likes it hot as well.

Site early spring-flowering plants such as evergreen azaleas, *Ledum* and *Pieris* away from an easterly aspect (or a westerly one, if you live in the southern hemisphere). Ground frosts in spring followed by morning sun will destroy early blooms and young growths.

■ **Left** *Helianthemum* 'Rhodanthe Carneum' performs bests in a well-drained alkaline soil.

■ **Above right** *Diascia rigescens* will flower all summer long if dead flower stalks are removed.

■ **Right** Contrasting junipers, *Juniperus communis* 'Depressa' and *J. squamata* 'Blue Star' form a dense carpet, giving weeds no chance.

▼ **JOHN'S CHOICE**

*The rock rose (*Helianthemum *'Rhodanthe Carneum').*
Lots of gardeners will know this plant as Helianthemum *'Wisley Pink' and it is a favorite because it seems to flower all summer long in a most delightful shade of pink, each bloom shaded apricot yellow in the center. The leaves are silver gray and it will spread to about 18 in (45 cm).*

GOOD COMBINATION
Juniperus communis and *Taxus baccata* 'Repandens', both conifers capable of growing far and wide, making them ideal for large expanses that require quick, dense ground cover.

■ **Above** *Sedum spathulifolium* 'Cape Blanco' is a quick-covering alpine – even a broken piece or one dropped by the birds will readily take root.

■ **Right** A mixed planting of shrubs, herbaceous perennials, rhizomes, bulbs and conifers produces late spring color in a sunny border.

**FOR MORE DETAILS OF
ALL THESE PLANTS SEE
THE DIRECTORY ON
PAGES 92–154**

PLANTS BEST FOR FULL SUN

Conifers

Juniperus communis

Juniperus horizontalis

Juniperus procumbens

Juniperus squamata 'Blue Star'

Taxus baccata 'Repandens'

Herbs

Rosmarinus officinalis
  'Prostratus'

Thymus vulgaris

Alpines

Asarina procumbens

Genista procumbens

Helianthemum 'Rhodanthe
  Carneum'

Helianthemum 'Wisley
  Primrose'

Sedum spathulifolium

Herbaceous perennials

Cerastium tomentosum

Geranium endressii 'Wargrave
  Pink'

*Geranium sanguineum
  striatum*

Saponaria ocymoides

Persicaria affinis

Persicaria vacciniifolia

Shrubs

Cistus × *corbariensis*

Cistus × *cyprius*

Convolvulus cneorum

Cytisus × *praecox*

Genista lydia

Genista hispanica

Halimium ocymoides

PLANTS TOLERANT OF FULL SUN

Herb

Ruta graveolens

Herbaceous perennial

Diascia rigescens

SPECIAL SITUATIONS

BANKS AND TERRACES

Banks raise the level of interest – horticulturally rather than financially in this case, although they do have advantages and disadvantages in the garden, a sort of profit and loss. Banks may be referred to as slopes, gradients, changes of level or terraces, but the word 'bank' seems, somehow or other, to sum them up.

The first thing to find out when looking for plants for a bank is whether it is facing the house or falling away from it. If seen from the dwelling the planting needs to be interesting, with year-round color, and generally more ornamental than if it falls away offering no display to the windows. Of course if the bank is facing the main road or other houses in plain view then, with due respect to the Jones's, it needs to look good.

A change of level is an advantage in any garden, helping to create interest and structure. However, unless it is carefully designed, it can result in extra hours of maintenance – and a sore back and legs. There are lots of problems including soil erosion, surface water, summer drought, poor access and subsoil coming through to the surface of a bank. If the surface is reasonably stable and the slope is not steep it should be possible to cultivate lightly to provide a tilth which will encourage plants to grow and spread. Steeper banks may require pit planting, preceded by spraying to kill weeds and grass, leaving the dead vegetation to help hold the soil and prevent erosion until the planting becomes established. The sward can simply be

▼ JOHN'S CHOICE

Hebe pinguifolia *'Pagei'. This is a plant that won't let you down. It can tolerate a whole range of conditions and will spread to cover almost 9 square feet (about a square meter). The snow-white flowers are carried in late spring and early summer just above the small blue-green leaves.*

■ **Left** Senecio and honeysuckle tumbling over a retaining wall with *Sedum spectabile*, geranium, convolvulus, calceolaria and the Irish yew *Taxus baccata variegata* 'Aurea' in the foreground.

Above right Tender *Convolvulus cneorum* likes a well-drained soil in full sun. Its gray foliage looks good even when it is not in flower.

■ **Right** *Euonymus fortunei* 'Emerald Gaiety' does best in poor soil, but must have full sun.

PLANTS BEST FOR TERRACES

Heathers

Calluna vulgaris

Erica carnea

Alpine

Helianthemum apenninum

Shrubs

Convolvulus cneorum

Cotoneaster dammeri

Hebe pinguifolia 'Pagei'

PLANTS TOLERANT OF TERRACES

Shrubs

Euonymus 'Emerald 'n' Gold'

Euonymus 'Emerald Gaiety'

Hebe albicans

Senecio 'Sunshine'

GOOD COMBINATION

Convolvulus cneorum and *Euonymus* 'Emerald 'n' Gold' planted together produce a pleasing mixture of leaf colors, the silvery gray of the convolvulus contrasting with the bright green and yellow variegation of euonymus.

---

treated with a translocated weedkiller containing glyphosate. The grass will be effectively killed, although grass weeds such as plantain, buttercup and daisy may need a second application or a specific lawn weed killer.

Pit planting involves no overall cultivation, simply holes dug where the plants are to be grown. Dig the planting hole larger than necessary to accommodate the roots, fork up the bottom of the pit, mix in some compost and slow-release fertilizer and plant firmly. Leave the finished soil level slightly depressed to hold water until it soaks into the soil rather than run off the surface leaving the plant roots dry.

It is more difficult for plants with stolons or suckers, or those that stem-layer as they grow, to get their young roots into the hard uncultivated

soil. Plants with stiff woody branches that tend to spread over the ground – such as ground-hugging cotoneasters and junipers – are particularly useful for holding soil firmly in place and preventing erosion. Both will spread horizontally to cover large areas.

Some of the traditional twining rather than suckering climbers will cover a bank if given a support to scramble over. Galvanised wire mesh spread over the bank and firmly secured – using galvanised hoops of wire pushed into the soil or tied with galvanised wire to wooden pegs driven into the bank – is an ideal method of support. Plant clematis, honeysuckle, or climbing or rambling roses. After planting water the roots in well to avoid checking the plants and to encourage rapid growth. Train the new shoots through the wire mesh to ensure that they are securely held. Once

■ **Above left** *Hebe pinguifolia* 'Pagei' flowers in late spring and early summer.

■ **Above** Tumbling water and tumbling plants complement each other in a tropical setting.

■ **Right** *Euonymus* 'Emerald 'n' Gold' forms a dense evergreen mat.

FOR MORE DETAILS OF
ALL THESE PLANTS SEE
THE DIRECTORY ON
PAGES 92–154

PLANTS BEST FOR STEEP BANKS
Climber
Hedera canariensis
Conifers
Juniperus conferta
Juniperus repanda
Alpine
Aurinia saxatilis 'Citrina'
Herbaceous perennials
Ajuga reptans 'Burgundy Glow'
Artemisia schmidtiana
Centranthus ruber
Lamium maculatum 'White Nancy'
Shrubs
Rubus tricolor
Vinca major
Vinca minor 'Azurea Flore Pleno'

PLANTS TOLERANT OF STEEP BANKS
Alpine
Arabis caucasica 'Variegata'
Shrubs
Hypericum calycinum
Hypericum empetrifolium

GOOD COMBINATION
Ajuga reptans 'Burgundy Glow' and *Vinca minor* 'Azurea Flore Pleno'. These two friends have proved themselves time and time again, producing cover and color on the worst of banks without needing lots of maintenance.

SPECIAL SITUATIONS

they are attached and growing strongly they will reward you with masses of bloom. You can bank on it.

A bank can be formed into a rockery provided you use a bit of taste and actually build a proper rockery with the rock 'growing' out of the ground with most of the rock below the soil surface. If the rock has strata lines they should all be running the same way, just as they do in nature. The rocks should be placed close together with small pockets of soil to accommodate the plants. The alternative is often seen and best described as a stonery with stones like raisins in a bread pudding.

It is important that all, and I mean all, perennial weeds are removed prior to constructing a rockery or planting out. Murphy's law states that the roots of the one noxious perennial weed that was left will be under the biggest stone, or in the middle of a choice plant that won't enjoy either its presence or the root disturbance that comes when you remove the weed. Clambering about a sloping rockery like a mountain goat is good exercise, but then so is a brisk walk around the garden.

Banks that slope away from the house or main viewing point can be made interesting by bringing the plants over the top of the bank on to the level surface. This is especially successful where a lawn runs to the bank. Allowing the planted area to encroach into the lawn will shorten the horizon, make it visually more interesting and suggest that there is more beyond, especially if you use low-growing plants. In the same way a steep bank will look less severe when viewed from below if the planting is carried beyond the base of the bank on to the level ground. Curving the front of the bed rather than finishing it abruptly with a straight line will give an appearance of depth, and of the natural spread of the plants.

A series of lawned terraces looks very aristocratic, especially just after they have been nicely cut, but grass will revert to its peasant ways long before it gets its next trim. Unless the slope is very gradual and the terraces wide, it is difficult and dangerous to trim across. A hover mower is usually used for cutting and if the bank is steep or long the mower can be controlled with a rope from the top of the terrace, pulled up and allowed to slide down – a real labor of love. Pit-planted ground cover will remove the necessity for mowing altogether. If the planting takes place with the minimum of soil disturbance there will be fewer weed seeds turned up to germinate and the plants can establish and form cover before further weed seedlings appear.

■ **Left** *Aurinia saxatilis* 'Citrina' should be clipped back after flowering to stop it becoming leggy.

■ **Right** *Lamium maculatum* 'White Nancy' – a refined form of lamium, easily kept under control.

■ **Right** *Hypericum empetrifolium* is not suitable for a sunless bank, but in the right conditions it will flower continuously all summer.

▼ **JOHN'S CHOICE**

Aurinia saxatilis '*Citrina*', *sometimes known as gold dust, used to be called* Alyssum saxatile *and makes a great show in late spring and early summer with its panicles of bright, lemon-yellow flowers. Cutting back with shears after flowering will thicken the plant up and prevent it becoming straggly. The variety* 'Dudley Nevill' *has yellow-orange blooms. A. s.* Variegata *is a variegated form with pale cream margins to the leaves.*

SPECIAL SITUATIONS

WOODLAND

Woodlands and copses are a form of ground cover in their own right, albeit tall cover. Fewer weeds germinate and thrive in the shade of tree canopies. Where a second, lower layer of ground cover can also be established, weed population drops still further, providing a minimum maintenance regime. Where the canopy of leaves is broken, glade areas permit plants that require more light to be planted, especially those with evergreen or variegated leaves. Evergreen plants are more susceptible to damage from autumn leaf fall than deciduous plants and it may be necessary to rake, brush or blow deep layers of large, decomposing leaves off some plants.

▼ JOHN'S CHOICE

Trillium grandiflorum *will spread to 18 in (45 cm) and reach a similar height. The dark green leaves are up to 12 in (30 cm) long and in spring and summer large white flowers are produced just above the foliage. They fade to pink, contrasting with the green sepals. The variety* T. grandiflorum *'Flore Pleno' has double blooms.*

■ **Left** *Daphne laureola* is a great woodland evergreen, succeeding even in deep shade.

■ **Above** *Trillium grandiflorum,* the wake robin, will grow quickly to form a clump.

■ **Right** It is unusual to see *Pachysandra terminalis* with berries such as these. In a moist, open soil it will spread rapidly by underground stems, producing masses of the familiar white flowers.

PLANTS SUITABLE FOR WOODLAND

Fern
Polystichum aculeatum

Rhizomes
Arisarum proboscideum
Trillium grandiflorum

Herbaceous perennials
Asarum caudatum
Geranium macrorrhizum
    'Ingwersen's Variety'
Hosta fortunei
Pachysandra terminalis
Tiarella cordifolia

Shrubs
Aucuba japonica 'Rozannie'
Daphne laureola
Skimmia japonica 'Fructo-alba'
Vinca major

PLANTS TOLERANT OF WOODLAND
Shrubs
Buxus sempervirens
    'Suffruticosa'
Lonicera pileata
Mahonia nervosa
Rubus tricolor
Sarcococca confusa

GOOD COMBINATION

Aucuba japonica 'Rozannie' and *Daphne laureola* grow to about the same height and both are evergreen. 'Rozannie' is bisexual, producing red berries in autumn and winter; the daphne has fragrant greenish flowers, followed by red berries.

FOR MORE DETAILS OF ALL THESE PLANTS SEE THE DIRECTORY ON PAGES 92–154

■ **Top** *Skimmia japonica* 'Nymans' – a free-fruiting clone with remarkably large red berries.

■ **Above** *Primula vulgaris*, the primrose, is everyone's favorite and is at home on a shady bank or open woodland.

■ **Right** Woodland designed to be enjoyed. Ferns, primula, *Acer palmatum* and hosta flourishing in dappled shade.

SPECIAL SITUATIONS

ALKALINE SITES

Some soils are just on the limy or alkaline side of neutral and are capable of growing a wide range of plants. Many acid-loving plants can survive, but the excess lime will lock up trace elements such as iron and magnesium, giving the plants a stunted, chlorotic appearance with mottled and yellow leaves.

Soils that form a thin layer over chalk restrict plant selection not only to those that like a high pH, but also to those tolerant of drought. Limy soils are usually shallow, stony and very well drained, warming up quickly in spring. Generous mulching will increase the depth and quality of soil and help retain moisture. The addition of peat or ericaceous compost will lower the pH, allowing a wider range of plants to be grown. However, deep-rooted, lime-hating shrubs and trees such as holly and berberis species will be unable to thrive.

▼ JOHN'S CHOICE

Sarcococca humilis, *sometimes called Christmas box or sweet box , is a very adaptable evergreen plant tolerating shade and total neglect. The white flowers, produced in winter, are tinged with pink, deliciously fragrant, and are followed by blue-black berries. Spreading by suckers this superb plant will grow to a height of 24 in (60 cm) with a 4 ft (1.2 m) spread.*

GOOD COMBINATION

Santolina pinnata neapolitana and *Choisya* 'Aztec Pearl' both have aromatic foliage. If the taller choisya is planted behind the santolina the contrast of leaf shape and color is eye-catching. 'Aztec Pearl' flowers white in late spring and again in late summer and autumn and the small, yellow, button flowers of *Santolina* appear in late summer.

■ **Left** *Sarcococca humilis* loves deep shade, filling the air with its fragrance in the dead of winter.

■ **Right** *Choisya* 'Aztec Pearl' is a compact evergreen shrub, easy to grow and forming good, dense cover.

PLANTS BEST FOR ALKALINE SOILS

Alpine
Euphorbia myrsinites

Herbaceous perennials
Bergenia cordifolia 'Purpurea'
Viola cornuta

Shrubs
Santolina pinnata neapolitana
Sarcococca humilis

PLANTS TOLERANT OF ALKALINE SOILS

Shrubs
Choisya 'Aztec Pearl'
Jasminum fruticans

FOR MORE DETAILS OF ALL THESE PLANTS SEE THE DIRECTORY ON PAGES 92-154

■ **Above** *Euphorbia myrsinites* has succulent foliage and needs to be grown in full sun. Its striking graphic shape makes an unusual striking feature in the middle of a gravel path.

■ **Right** *Bergenia cordifolia* 'Purpurea' flowers in late winter and early spring.

■ **Opposite** *Santolina pinnata neapolitana* does best in well-drained soil in full sun.

SPECIAL SITUATIONS

SPECIAL SITUATIONS

ACID SITES

Acid soils are often quite dark and rich in organic material, the best examples being peat, or woodland soils where years of leaf litter have built up a deep, humus-rich surface layer of soil. Clay soils are usually acid and retentive of moisture, requiring drainage and the addition of grit or coarse sand to make them more manageable. Such soils may be 'late' – slow to warm up at the start of the season – but if well cultivated they are ideal for all those lime-hating ground-covering plants such as *Calluna, Rhododendron, Erica, Skimmia, Ledum* and *Gaultheria*. Sandy, free-draining soils can also be acid and are often lacking in nutrients, which are leached down below the level of the roots. Adding lots of compost and well-rotted farmyard manure will make the soil more moisture-retentive. *Ilex crenata*, helianthemums and all the juniper family will thrive in this sort of soil.

▼ JOHN'S CHOICE

Lithodora diffusa *'Heavenly Blue' used to be named* Lithospermum diffusum *'Heavenly Blue' and thank goodness only the name changed. It loves an acid soil rich in humus and will then produce a sheet of deep blue flowers which almost cover its evergreen dark green leaves in late spring and early summer. It will spread to over 24 in (60 cm).*

GOOD COMBINATION

Lithodora diffusa 'I leavenly Blue' and *Pieris japonica* 'Little Heath' are quite happy together, with the lithodora providing sheets of blue under the pieris, whose pink-tinged leaves are margined with silver.

■ **Opposite** *Lithodora diffusa* 'Heavenly Blue' is great for ground cover but hates limy soil.

■ **Left** *Daboecia cantabrica* is a heather-like shrub, forming solid sheets of color in summer and early autumn.

FOR MORE DETAILS OF ALL THESE PLANTS SEE THE DIRECTORY ON PAGES 92–154

PLANTS BEST FOR ACID SOILS

Fern

Adiantum pedatum

Heathers

Calluna vulgaris

Erica cinerea

Alpines

Celmisia walkeri

Phlox stolonifera

Lithodora diffusa 'Heavenly Blue'

Herbaceous perennial

Gentiana x *macaulayi*

Shrubs

Daboecia cantabrica

Pieris japonica 'Little Heath'

Rhododendron

PLANTS TOLERANT OF ACID SOILS

Heather

Daboecia cantabrica

Herbaceous perennial

Smilacina racemosa

■ **Above right** *Phlox stolonifera*, the creeping phlox, enjoys well-drained soil in semi-shade.

■ **Right** *Erica cinerea* 'Alba Minor' will flower from summer through to early autumn.

■ **Opposite** *Adiantum pedatum* is deciduous, the fronds appearing early in spring. It is one of my favorite ferns because the divided leaves allow light to penetrate to the undergrowth.

SPECIAL SITUATIONS

HEAVY CLAY SOIL

More gardeners complain of trying to garden on heavy, sticky clay than on any other soil type. Often the problem has less to do with the geography of the site than with the builder who stripped the topsoil and, instead of stockpiling it to put it back when the work was finished, sold it to another gardener in an equally new site of clay and rubble, who now marvels at the quality of the soil and the difference it makes to his garden. Hence the expression 'imported' topsoil – which is not foreign at all, it just comes from up the road.

▼ JOHN'S CHOICE

Viburnum davidii. *Of all the viburnums this one stands out for foliage. To see the weak winter sunlight playing on the dark green leaves with their three deep veins is magic. Small white flowers in spring are followed by metallic blue berries that are ovoid in shape. A word of caution, however – both male and female plants are required if berries are to be produced.*

PLANTS BEST FOR HEAVY CLAY SOILS

Conifer

Pinus mugo 'Mops'

Herb

Mentha longifolia

Herbaceous perennials

Geranium macrorrhizum

Houttuynia cordata 'Chamaeleon'

Pulmonaria saccharata

Shrubs

Chaenomeles × superba

Cytisus × praecox 'All Gold'

Potentilla fruticosa 'Manchu'

Skimmia × confusa 'Kew Green'

Viburnum davidii

PLANTS TOLERANT OF CLAY SOILS

Herbaceous perennial

Rodgersia podophylla

Shrubs

Aucuba japonica 'Crotonifolia'

Choisya ternata

Rubus tricolor

GOOD COMBINATION

Viburnum davidii and *Pinus mugo* 'Mops' are both evergreen and their foliage provides a complete contrast between large, glossy leaves and dull green needles.

■ **Opposite** The young foliage of *Rodgersia podophylla* is bronze, becoming mid-green as the season progresses and finally turning bronze-red in autumn.

■ **Left** *Chaenomeles × superba* flowers from spring to early summer.

Whatever the reason, heavy clay can be horrible to work with, wet and sticky in winter, then baked hard and cracked in summer. The addition of lashings of compost, old rotted manure or leaf mould and incorporating coarse grit will open the clay up and break down the lumps to a crumbly soil that is ideal for plant growth. The good news is that clay soils are usually extremely fertile, with all the trace elements necessary to produce healthy plants.

It is not good practice to pit-plant into a clay soil any plants that have a weak or deeply penetrating root system, as the hard surrounding clay will act in the same way as a plastic pot, restricting the roots to the 'pit' of worked soil. Make as large a hole as possible, fork up the base of the hole, add grit or compost and plant strong-growing plants with shallow roots that spread at or just below ground level like mint or *Pinus mugo* 'Mops'.

There is no shortage of plants that enjoy clay soils and given a little Tender Loving Care early on they will not only survive but really thrive on your worst nightmare of clay.

SPECIAL SITUATIONS

■ **Opposite above**
Viburnum davidii has flowers,
fruit and attractive evergreen
foliage.

■ **Opposite below** *Aucuba
japonica* 'Crotonifolia' provides
a splash of color throughout
the year.

■ **Left** *Pinus mugo* 'Mops' – a
great dwarf pine for dense
cover.

**FOR MORE DETAILS OF
ALL THESE PLANTS SEE
THE DIRECTORY ON
PAGES 92–154**

SPECIAL SITUATIONS

DRY SANDY SOIL

A friend once said that his soil was only fit for camels but we were walking around his garden at the time and it was crammed with plants and splashed with color.

Dry, light, open soils are not moisture-retentive, and are low in nutrients and humus, but to their advantage they are easily cultivated all year round and they warm up early in the season. It is actually enjoyable hoeing weeds growing in a sandy soil because they uproot so easily.

Working masses of humus into the soil will gradually improve its structure and help retain moisture. Surface mulches will also help, but the worm population is lower in sandy soil, so you can't rely on them to transport the mulch down into the ground. Only apply granular fertilizers to moist soils because the plant roots take the nutrients up in liquid form. A liquid or foliar feed will have more immediate results.

▼ JOHN'S CHOICE

Cistus x *purpureus, the sun rose or rock rose, is my favorite cistus. I love them all, but* purpureus *was the first species that I grew and I like its wavy leaves, red stems and large dark pink flowers with the maroon blotches at the base of each of the three petals. Flowering in summer, the blooms look like the paper flowers that gypsies used to sell.*

PLANTS BEST FOR DRY SANDY SOILS

Herbaceous perennials

Erigeron 'Charity'

Osteospermum jucundum

Shrubs

Ballota acetabulosa

Brachyglottis compacta

Cistus x *purpureus*

Cytisus x *praecox*

Potentilla fruticosa 'Manchu '

PLANTS TOLERANT OF SANDY SOIL

Shrubs

Potentilla fruticosa 'Tilford Cream'

Santolina chamaecyparissus

■ **Left** *Ballota acetabulosa* can be pruned in mid-spring to keep it compact.

■ **Right** *Potentilla fruticosa* 'Tilford Cream' is a dense, spreading plant, flowering from late spring until early autumn.

GOOD COMBINATION

Ballota acetabulosa and *Potentilla fruticosa* 'Tilford Cream' make a good combination of evergreen and deciduous leaves with the ballota plants dotted through the potentilla. Alternatively, if the ballota is planted in front, it will screen the potentilla's untidy winter appearance. The purple-pink and cream flowers blend well.

FOR MORE DETAILS OF ALL THESE PLANTS SEE THE DIRECTORY ON PAGES 92–154

■ **Below** *Santolina chamaecyparissus* is often known as the cotton lavender because of its fluffy appearance. It provides aromatic foliage all year, with button-like yellow flowers in mid- to late summer.

Coastal soils are often thought of as sandy, but they can also be either stony, rocky, marshy, heavy clay or have thin soil overlying chalk. The one thing that all coastal sites have in common is onshore winds that are laden with salt. The salt is deposited on leaves and young shoots, causing permanent scorching or death. Plants with small leaves such as some of the hebes have a reduced surface area for the salty deposits to gather on and plants with shiny, leathery leaves like those of eleagnus allow the salt to be washed off by winter rain.

■ **Right** *Cistus* x *purpureus* can be short-lived, but I love it every minute I have it.

■ **Opposite** *Brachyglottis compacta* 'Sunshine' makes a good windbreak in coastal gardens. .

SPECIAL SITUATIONS

EXPOSED SITES

By now even the most reluctant gardener must have realized that there are many different soil types and climatic conditions and that a combination of these can be to your advantage, or work against you to the point where you are ready to construct the smallest concrete airport runway in the country. I have bad news for you. There is one more site that is fraught with difficulties – the exposed garden. By exposed I mean an area that is open to the elements and that includes cold, biting winds, the glare of full sun, frost and snow.

The good news is that, as I have shown with other types of site, provided you are aware of the problems you will be able to choose ground-cover plants that will tolerate or even thrive in what appear to be horrible conditions. There are a few rules to stick to, however, to give your plants a good start and number one is to plant them out in their permanent positions after the worst of the bad weather is over. A good feed of liquid fertilizer at the start of the growing season will help, and if your garden is subject to very cold weather in winter a feed high in potash in autumn will harden the young shoots. Evergreen shrubs are more susceptible to damage in winter than deciduous plants, since they are still active and growing.

It is possible to succeed with a wider range of ground-covering plants by creating a more conducive habitat through the use of windbreaks and shelter belts. Temporary shelter can be provided until the plants become established or acclimatised, or, if space permits, you can make a perimeter planting of species such as *Bupleurum fruticosum* and *Elaeagnus* x *ebbingei* 'Limelight' that are tolerant of the conditions. The more desirable landscaping can then be planted on the sheltered side. On windy sites, you may need to support taller plants with stakes and ties. Firm the plant roots into the soil after heavy frosts have broken up the surface, especially where low plants such as periwinkle are spread by runners. Here it may be a good idea to peg the shoots down with stones or, better still, short pieces of wire bent into hoops to keep them in place until they root. Otherwise, strong winds will keep them on the move and prevent them from anchoring firmly into the surface.

In the northern hemisphere, ground-covering plants at the base of south-facing walls are very likely to dry out in summer (the same is, of course, true of north-facing walls in the southern hemisphere). The walls draw in available moisture and the eaves of the house prevent rainfall from reaching the soil and at the same time the sun, when it appears, is at its hottest. Lots of compost dug into the soil and surface mulches will help to retain moisture.

▼ **JOHN'S CHOICE**

Hebe x franciscana *is a great plant for use at the seaside. Evergreen with fleshy, dull green leaves and purple flowers during summer and autumn, it is a compact shrub that can also be used as a low hedge.*

■ **Opposite** *Escallonia* 'Pride of Donard' has shiny evergreen leaves and flowers in early summer.

■ **Above** *Centranthus ruber* will tolerate exposure, even growing out of the cracks in walls.

■ **Right** *Olearia* × *haastii*, the daisy bush, grows well at the seaside.

■ **Below left** The silvery foliage of *Anthemis punctata cupaniana* turns green in winter.

■ **Below right** *Catananche caerulea* can put up with anything, even gale-force winds.

■ **Opposite** Striking in flower and foliage, the sea holly *Eryngium alpinum* tolerates all but waterlogged conditions.

PLANTS BEST FOR EXPOSED SITES

Herbaceous perennials

Anthemis punctata cupaniana

Centranthus ruber

Eryngium alpinum

Kniphofia ensifolia

Shrubs

Escallonia 'Pride of Donard'

Hebe × franciscana

PLANTS TOLERANT OF EXPOSED SITES

Herbaceous perennials

Agapanthus 'Dorothy Palmer'

Catananche caerulea

Centaurea cineraria

Shrubs

Bupleurum fruticosum

Elaeagnus × ebbingei

Olearia × haastii

GOOD COMBINATION

Escallonia 'Pride of Donard' and *Olearia × haastii*. Both are evergreen, the escallonia with shiny dark green leaves and red flowers in mid-summer, the olearia also with dark green foliage but with daisy-like white flowers appearing after the escallonia, in late summer. Two tough shrubs guaranteed to flower.

FOR MORE DETAILS OF ALL THESE PLANTS SEE THE DIRECTORY ON PAGES 92–154

SPECIAL SITUATIONS

UNDER HEDGES

Where low-growing carpeting plants are required at the base of hedges, great care needs to be taken in choosing species. Usually the soil is impoverished, the roots of the hedge having depleted the ground of nutrients. An established hedge will continue to grow by sending its roots deep into the subsoil in search of food and moisture. For this reason the soil at the base of the hedges is likely to be bone dry and even when it does rain the overhanging leaf cover acts as an umbrella, throwing the water well out beyond the sides of the hedge. Most of the food and water you provide for your ground-cover plants will be taken by the hedge, encouraging excess growth, so it is more sensible to choose plants like those listed below that can tolerate the dry, poor soil that they have inherited.

▼ JOHN'S CHOICE

The golden male fern Dryopteris affinis *is virtually evergreen, especially under a sheltered hedge. In spring the unfurling fronds are pale green, contrasting with the golden mid-brown ribs. By autumn the fronds are dark green and 36 in (90 cm) high.*

PLANTS BEST FOR UNDER HEDGES

Ferns

Althyrium filix-femina

Dryopteris affinis

Polystichum setiferum

Corm

Crocosmia 'Solfaterre'

Herbaceous perennial

Euphorbia robbiae

PLANTS TOLERANT OF UNDER HEDGES

Herbaceous perennials

Anemone × hybrida

Campanula latifolia 'Prichards Variety'

Shrub

Vinca major

■ **Left** Unlike the stronger-growing red crocosmias, *C. solfaterre* is of compact habit and not fully hardy.

■ **Right** *Euphorbia robbiae*, loved by flower arrangers for its greenish yellow 'flowers'.

GOOD COMBINATION

Crocosmia 'Solfaterre' and *Euphorbia robbiae* grow to approximately 24 in (60 cm). The euphorbia is a rapidly spreading evergreen with dark green leathery foliage and greenish yellow 'flowers' in late spring and early summer. *Crocosmia* 'Solfaterre' has attractive lance-shaped bronze foliage that dies away in autumn and apricot yellow flowers in summer. Together they provide interest all year round.

FOR MORE DETAILS OF ALL THESE PLANTS SEE THE DIRECTORY ON PAGES 92-154

SPECIAL SITUATIONS

PATIOS AND PATHS

Hard surface areas such as paved or gravel paths or patios are usually thought of as minimum maintenance areas and it is only when planting is introduced to them that the additional maintenance work required becomes evident. However, looking after some planted areas is usually worth the extra effort just to soften large masses of paving or other solid surfaces. Straight edges and defined boundaries can be broken up, allowing prostrate and creepy-crawly ground-huggers to spread over the surface.

Before planting or even purchasing your plants check that they won't be too rampant, scampering over the patio and eventually burying it under a carpet of twiggy, wiry stems. *Cotoneaster* 'Skogholm' and *Rubus tricolor* come to mind as two plants that are quite capable of making a patio

▼ JOHN'S CHOICE

Gentiana verna *is sometimes referred to as the spring gentian and presents a carpet of sky-blue, tubular flowers in spring or early summer over dark evergreen leaves. Unfortunately it is often a short-lived plant but is well worth replacing.*

PLANTS BEST FOR PATIOS AND PATHS

Herb

Thymus serpyllum

Alpines

Aubretia × *cultorum* 'Argenteovariegata'

Aurinia saxatalis 'Citrina'

Dianthus

Gentiana verna

Herbaceous perennials

Geranium endressii

Persicaria vacciniifolium

Phlox douglasii

PLANTS TOLERANT OF PATIOS AND PATHS

Herbaceous perennials

Artemesia schmidtiana

Saxifraga 'Southside Seedling'

■ **Opposite** *Phlox douglasii* enjoys well-drained soil in full sun and is a most reliable plant.

■ **Left** *Geranium endressii* is a great perennial for edging patios and paths.

disappear in a flash, or certainly in a season or two. Paths can also be made more interesting by softening their edges, or planting small-leaved, compact-growing plants such as *Thymus serpyllum* into the gravel or between the cracks in the slabs. All the varieties of thyme are ideal for crevice-filling, providing aroma, flower and a wide range of leaf color.

Where broken paving or flat slabs of rock are used to form hard surfaces the gaps are usually grouted with a cement/sand mix. If some random areas are left ungrouted a gritty mixture of soil can be used to fill the spaces which can then be planted with flat-growing scented plants such as chamomile that can tolerate being walked upon, releasing their aroma under the pressure of your feet. On a calm summer's evening such a path can evoke long-lost memories.

With small patios where space is at a premium it is not a good idea to remove slabs at random for planting up, as this restricts both movement and the use of garden furniture. Simply plant around the perimeter of the patio and allow the plants to grow inwards, softening the edges.

■ **Right** A generous planting of *Dianthus* softens the hard surfaces of stepping stones, sleepers and gravel, enjoying the dry, sunny conditions.

■ **Below** *Saxifraga* 'Southside Seedling' is mat-forming and flowers in late spring and early summer.

■ **Opposite** A secret garden carpeted with lambs' ears, mint, thyme and hosta. Clipped box adds shape and texture.

■ **Above** A pattern of stone and moss in the courtyard of Tokufuji Temple in Kyoto, Japan.

■ **Left** *Gentiana verna* forms an evergreen mat. Sadly, it is often short-lived.

FOR MORE DETAILS OF ALL THESE PLANTS SEE THE DIRECTORY ON PAGES 92–154

FORMAL GARDENS

They say that there is nothing new under the sun and when it comes to the design of formal gardens this is certainly true. Knot or knotte gardens – formed by planting low hedges in intricate patterns, usually interweaving and comparatively informal – have been with us since Elizabethan times and have changed little over the centuries, although varieties of plants have greatly improved. Parterres, which originated in France and are more formal, with dwarf plants forming rectangular patterns, became popular in Britain in the Victorian and Edwardian periods.

Many of the early knot gardens used gravel, brick, cobbles or even clinker ash from the hothouse boilers of the big house to color in and surface the beds formed between the dwarf hedges that were usually of box. Later, local authority parks departments planted elaborate parterres, using annuals on a massive scale to form huge colorful displays. Today ground-covering plants are in demand for this sort of design, provided

▼ **JOHN'S CHOICE**
For good mixtures of leaf and flower color Ajuga, Persicaria, Alchemilla *and* Ageratum *all combine to make a good design.*

■ **Opposite** Box hedging interplanted with a selection of sages (*Salvia officinalis*).

■ **Below** An intricate design that needs regular clipping if it is to maintain its elegant shape.

GOOD COMBINATION
Each defined area usually has a mass planting of one species and one color. The areas are separated by low hedges, often of *Buxus*.

PLANTS BEST FOR FORMAL GARDENS
Heather
Calluna vulgaris 'Alba Rigida'
Herbaceous perennials
Ajuga reptans 'Multicolor'
Pachysandra terminalis 'Green Carpet'
Pachysandra terminalis 'Variegata'
Persicaria vaccinifolia

PLANTS TOLERANT OF FORMAL GARDENS

Herb
Thymus serpyllum 'Pink Chintz'
Alpine
Alchemilla alpina
Shrubs
Daphne cneorum
Santolina chamaecyparissus
Vinca minor variegata

they are not so vigorous as to escape from their plot, thus spoiling the pattern. A selection of plants to give a subtly colored effect may include *Ajuga, Vinca*, heathers, *Pachysandra* and *Santolina*. Left to set their own limits each and every one of these will quickly travel beyond its allotted space, but an annual pruning will teach them some manners and curtail their urge to explore.

Formal gardens with intricate patterns are best viewed from above, so if you haven't got a castle or even a two-storey house it is best to site your knot garden or parterre at the bottom of a slope. Maintenance is remarkably easy once the cover is complete, leaving clipping of the formal dwarf hedging the only regular task.

**FOR MORE DETAILS OF
ALL THESE PLANTS SEE
THE DIRECTORY ON
PAGES 92–154**

■ **Above** Spring bedding lends color to a formal terraced garden in Italy, complete with colored gravel and box topiary.

■ **Right** Formal box hedging round a vegetable bed struggles in vain to contain a very informal marrow.

SPECIAL SITUATIONS

SWIMMING POOLS AND TENNIS COURTS

Quite often it is desirable to have an area of soft landscaping in the vicinity of a swimming pool to soften the traditional paved zone that surrounds it. Grass is not ideal close to the water as some of the mowings are inevitably carried into the water by wind or bare feet, and will necessitate daily hoovering to remove them. For obvious reasons, thorny and spiky-leaved plants are not recommended either. Evergreen material will provide year-round structure without dying leaves blowing into the pool, and quick-growing plants to cover the bare soil are a must. The design should also allow for some plants that will appear to raise the temperature such as the cabbage palm (*Cordyline australis*). If the pool is in full sun lavenders, cistus and helianthemums will all do well.

Tennis courts are, for some obscure reason, often built into the side of sloping land, resulting in a steep bank at one end and partly around two sides. Such banks are difficult to maintain as mown grass and yet the grass has to be

▼ JOHN'S CHOICE
Hedera hibernica *is the Irish ivy and, as I have mentioned before, it is called that because it is one of the best! The leaves are dark green and it is capable of covering large areas of ground, but it has a bad habit of climbing anything it comes across.*

■ **Opposite** A well-landscaped pool surround with the emphasis on summer and autumn color.

■ **Below** *Erica carnea* 'Springwood White' is low-growing and can tolerate a lot of tramping over if you have to retrieve tennis balls.

PLANTS BEST FOR AROUND SWIMMING POOLS AND TENNIS COURTS

Climber
Hedera hibernica

Alpine
Helianthemum

Herbaceous perennials
Aegopodium podagraria 'Variegata'
Ajuga

Shrub
Vinca major

PLANTS TOLERANT OF AREAS AROUND SWIMMING POOLS AND TENNIS COURTS

Heather
Erica carnea 'Springwood White'

Shrubs
Cotoneaster dammeri
Cotoneaster 'Skogholm'

GOOD COMBINATION
Helianthemum 'Wisley Primrose' and *Erica carnea* 'Springwood White' provide late spring color that will live in your memory. Low-growing and evergreen, their combination of yellow and white flowers are great spring colors.

■ **Opposite** A riot of ground covering for summer show – hostas, roses (tucked well away from bare feet), violas, campanulas, delphiniums, *Lychnis*, *Verbascum* and *Hypericum*.

■ **Right** *Helianthemum* 'Wisley Primrose' is a great rock rose with clear yellow flowers.

FOR MORE DETAILS OF ALL THESE PLANTS SEE THE DIRECTORY ON PAGES 92–154

kept short or balls cannot be found. In addition, there has never been a fence designed high enough to keep one of my lobs in. The answer is to plant the slope with extremely low-growing vegetation that won't conceal the ball and will withstand trampling and bashing with the racquet. A very forgiving plant that comes to mind is my old favorite, the variegated ground elder *Aegopodium podagraria* 'Variegata'. It tends to die down in winter and is not quite as aggressive as its big brother the green-leaved weed pest ground elder or bishop weed, but it still needs to be kept under control and well back from an all-weather surface.

Most other garden games pose no particular risk to landscape planting, although it is Murphy's law that any ball that goes out of play is sure to be lost in the densest or most prickly area of planting. Provided care is taken when retrieving the ball no harm will come to any but the most delicate of plant material.

DIRECTORY

DIRECTORY OF GROUND COVER PLANTS

■ LEFT A single *Kniphofia* growing through a ground covering of *Crocosmia* 'Lucifer'. RIGHT Bog garden featuring *Hosta sieboldii* and *Gunnera manicata*.

I have already suggested that there is an enormous range of material available for use as ground cover. I have excluded trees because although they form excellent cover, it is quite usual to have a further canopy of ground cover beneath the trees. Large evergreen trees can be such a barrier to light that even weeds find it difficult to flourish under their cover.

Nature can, with ease, make a liar out of one's best attempts at an accurate plant directory by allowing plants to grow bigger, spread further and flower weeks out of season. In most instances I have used descriptions that I feel I can stand by and have drawn on my own experience with the plants I have grown. Describing color has been a problem – the difference between what I call violet-blue, mauve or purple could rest on the age of the flower, the intensity of light or even the type of soil the plant is growing in.

Except in the case of plants with obvious and definite preferences, such as rhododendrons, azaleas and pieris with their dislike of alkaline soils, I have tried not to be dogmatic regarding soil type. Plants have the ability to adapt and succeed in soil and climatic conditions that are well removed from their ideal indigenous habitat – indeed, many plants can survive, succeed and even thrive in a wide range of habitats.

Where I have mentioned specific varieties of plants, there may well be others equally deserving of being listed, but as author I get to pick my favorites!

CLIMBERS

What a lovely descriptive term! Climbing, for me, sums up a whole range of beautiful plants that are at their best when draped over, or scrambling up, support. I would love to tell you about their magical qualities as companions for all sorts of unusual plants, but since this book is about ground cover I will restrict myself to their horizontal rather than vertical attributes.

I once had a sturdy Clematis montana *'Elizabeth' which had just about conquered the straining wire to an electricity pole. The weight proved too much in a storm and the whole lot collapsed down the wire to lie like a haystack around the base. It formed a mound about 10 ft (3 m) high and I left it to see what it would do. It formed an ever-growing heap that each May was solid with soft pink flowers and close up the fragrance was noticeable.*

The moral of the story is that lots of climbers are quite happy limbo-dancing beneath taller shrubs. Many so-called climbers speedily cover banks and while deciduous species are not awe-inspiring in winter they are no more so when perpendicular. Rambling and climbing roses are examples that will provide wonderful color in summer.

Evergreen climbers are obviously more successful. The ivies are probably the best ground-covering plants available, spreading rapidly over any type of soil. The evergreen Clematis armandii *enjoys a sheltered situation but can travel enormous distances. The honeysuckles have a lot going for them as ground coverers and include a few evergreen varieties: L.* japonica *and its varieties are all evergreen (semi-evergreen in exposed areas), great for perfume and can be really rampant. L.* japonica *has long been classed as a weed in parts of North America. I once saw a disused tennis court completely smothered by L. j. 'Halliana'. It had been planted to grow up the boundary fence, but had escaped to do its own thing. It deserved center court, as the summer perfume was overpowering.*

Actinidia kolomicta (zones 5-8)
Deciduous, woody-stemmed, twining climber that will spread to over 33 ft (10 m). The leaves are splashed creamy white and pink, especially mature leaves in full sun. The roots prefer a cool shady spot and will root by layering as they spread. A good plant for holding soil on a steep bank.

Campsis
A vigorous, deciduous, climbing genus; *Campsis radicans* (zones 5-9) will grow to over 70 ft (20 m), with large, tubular, orange-red flowers in mid-to late summer. It flowers more freely than *C. grandiflora* (zones 7-9) and is better suited to cooler conditions, but *C. grandiflora* is less rampant, growing to only 20 ft (6 m) with peach-orange flowers. *C. x*

Clematis cirrhosa 'Freckles'

tagliabuana 'Madame Galen' (zones 5-9) will succeed in cold sites but may be cut back by frost in winter. Remove any damaged growths in late spring.

Cissus striata (Tender)
Sometimes called Ivy of Uruguay, a fast-growing evergreen with tough tendrils spreading to 30 ft (10 m). The serrated leaves are shiny green, forming a dense carpet. Not fully hardy in cold sites and is a greedy feeder, doing best in a rich, fertile soil.

Cobaea scandens (Annual)
In colder climates this evergreen tendril climber is normally grown as an annual. It is a pity that it can't tolerate frost. The large, bell-shaped, fragrant flowers are green-yellow when they first open, turning purple with age. It will spread to 16 ft (5 m).

Clematis
Clematis armandii (zones 7-9) is a marvellous evergreen climber with large, leathery, shining green leaves and masses of small white flowers in early spring. As a special bonus the flowers are fragrant with the scent of almonds. It will grow in full sun or part shade, spreading to cover 16 ft (5 m), and any soil will suit.

Clematis cirrhosa (zones 7-9) is another good evergreen climber, flowering from mid-winter until spring with scented cream flowers. The blooms are small and less noticeable than the silky tassels that follow in late spring. The spread is similar to *C. armandii*, but *C. cirrhosa* is not as good as a ground coverer as the foliage is less robust.

Clematis macropetala (zones 6-9) is not a rampant spreader, covering about 10 ft (3 m), but it makes up for it with masses of growths. The light green leaves are deciduous, with a sheet of semi-double mauve flowers with pale centers in late spring and summer. The good news is that it doesn't require pruning.

Clematis montana (zones 6-9) is a very vigorous scrambler, having no difficulty covering 40 ft (12 m). It is deciduous with mid-green leaves and pure white flowers in late spring. The variety 'Elizabeth' has pale

Hydrangea anomala petiolaris

pink flowers with a scent of vanilla. *C. m.* 'Tetrarose' produces masses of deep pink blooms with bronze leaves and deep red stems. All the montanas enjoy a north-facing aspect (south-facing in the southern hemisphere), are not fussy about soil and don't require pruning.

Clematis tangutica (zones 6-9) is vigorous enough to form a dense carpet of twiggy stems with mid-green, deciduous leaves. Flowering in summer and early autumn, it carries masses of golden yellow lantern-shaped blooms. It will quickly spread to 20 ft (6 m) and performs beautifully on a sunny slope or bank.

Fallopia baldschuanica (zones 5-9)
Used to be called *Polygonum baldschuanicum* and is better known as Mile-a-minute or Russian vine. It lives up to its common names, spreading to enormous distances. It is deciduous, with clusters of tiny creamy white flowers with a hint of pink in late summer and autumn. It will tolerate dry soil that is low in nitrogen.

Hedera
Ivies are marvellous as ground-covering plants in that they are all evergreen and have the ability to creep, crawl, climb, scramble and most definitely take over any site into which they are introduced. While they prefer an alkaline soil, they are prepared to put up with just about any conditions short of a water-logged bog.

Hedera helix (zones 5-10) is sometimes referred to as common ivy and includes numerous varieties, all of which benefit from frequent pinching out by removing the tips of the young growths to encourage a good spread. The variety 'Green Ripple' spreads to 4 ft (1.5 m) and seems loath to climb, so is ideal as an underplanting beneath taller plants. H. h. 'Sulphurea' will spread quickly, covering up to 10 ft (3 m) with larger than normal leaves splashed with pale yellow.

Hedera hibernica (zones 6-10) is also known as *Hedera helix* 'Hibernica' or Irish ivy and is much more rampant than *H. helix*. Its glossy green leaves have paler veins. It will spread at least 20 ft (6 m) and it just loves shade.

Hedera canariensis (zones 7-10) and its variety 'Variegata' are noticeable for their very large leaves. They spread rapidly, rooting as they go.

Hedera colchica (zones 7-10) will grow to 65 ft (20 m) with pale green leaves without lobes. The leaves of *H. c.* 'Sulphur Heart' are mainly yellow with green edges and veins. *H. c.* 'Dentata Variegata' has larger green leaves with pale golden edges.

Hydrangea anomala ssp. petiolaris (zones 4-9)
Often referred to simply as *H. petiolaris*, this is a strong-growing deciduous scrambler that clings with the help of its aerial roots and covers up to 80 ft (25 m). The flowers appear during the summer as large heads of creamy white lace caps with mid-green leaves. It likes a moist rich soil. This is a very hardy plant that will succeed on sun-starved banks and deep shade.

Lonicera
The honeysuckles are mostly happy to lie down and spread over the ground but can become a tangled mass that requires regular thinning out. They will grow in full sun or in partial shade and love a deep, rich, well-drained soil. Evergreen varieties should be planted in the spring when the soil is warming up. Most honeysuckles are sweetly scented.

Lonicera henryi (zones 5-9) is a non-fragrant evergreen. It has shiny, dark green leaves and purple-red flowers with a yellow throat, produced in early summer and followed by deep purple berries. It will spread to 33 ft (10 m).

Lonicera hildebrandiana (zones 6-8) is not quite hardy but if you can get away with it it will spread to 30 ft (9 m). A fast-growing evergreen, it produces large heads of fragrant, creamy white flowers in summer. The flowers fade to orange and are followed by red berries.

Lonicera japonica (zones 4-10) 'Halliana' is a very vigorous, woody-stemmed scrambler, evergreen in mild regions, with fragrant white flowers that yellow with age. It will trail over the ground to cover 33 ft (10 m).

Lonicera periclymenum (zones 5-9) 'Belgica' is a vigorous, twining, deciduous variety

covering 13 ft (4 m). It is early flowering (whereas the variety 'Serotina' is late flowering). The blooms are pink with cream centers and are beautifully fragrant, especially in the evening. *L. p.* 'Graham Thomas' is also fragrant with white flowers turning to clear yellow as they age through summer and autumn.

Lonicera sempervirens (zones 4-9) is an evergreen honeysuckle which, has no perfume, but its orange-red, trumpet-shaped summer flowers make up for it. It will spread to 13 ft (4 m).

Parthenocissus tricuspidata (zones 4-8)
Often called Boston ivy, this is a deciduous climber that is happy to take off horizontally and cover 65ft (20 m). The bright green leaves are up to 8 in (20 cm) long and turn brilliant red in autumn, even in partial shade.

Passiflora
Passiflora caerulea (zones 6-9) is quite hardy and vigorous enough to cover 33 ft (10 m) in a very short time. The purple and white flowers, produced in summer, are followed by bright orange fruits that are edible but have an insipid taste. The variety 'Constance Elliot' produces fragrant white flowers but is slightly tender.

Passiflora. mollissima (Tender) will grow to 33ft (10 m) with pale pink summer flowers and long, yellow, edible fruit.

Solanum crispum (zones 8-10)
Also known as potato vine, this is a scrambling evergreen climber that tumbles over itself, covering 13 ft (4 m) and carrying large clusters of mauve-blue fragrant flowers with bright golden yellow stamens in summer. The variety 'Glasnevin' is the one to grow, with deep purple-blue flowers during summer and autumn.

Vitis coignetiae (zones 5-9)
A rampant deciduous vine that will easily cover 80 ft (25 m). The large, heart-shaped leaves turn deep red in autumn before falling. This decorative vine produces small bunches of black fruit that taste horrible!

FERNS

Ferns probably get less publicity than any other plants. One of the reasons for this is that they don't flower and so can't cash in on the 'saw it, liked it, bought it' market. In fact, they lost popularity at the end of the Victorian era and have struggled to make an impression ever since. This really is a shame as they are marvellous plants and score highly as ground cover.

Despite the lack of flowers, amongst their attributes I can list the striking beauty of the leaves or fronds. I can think of no other plant that comes close to the beauty of the young fronds uncurling like shuttlecocks in spring and arching magnificently all summer.

The royal fern (Osmunda regalis) prefers really moist ground, but all the others like a dry soil. They prefer shady sites and while they love a limy soil they can grow quite happily in acid conditions. Many ferns are evergreen and those that are not often turn shades of yellow and rich brown in autumn, giving a subdued brightness to the darkest corner. Propagation is from the brown spores produced in large quantities on the back of the frond. Sow them sparingly on moist, soil-less compost and cover with glass. Keep the seed tray shaded until germination, when the seedlings appear like moss on the surface. Transplant as soon as the first true leaf has formed. Keep the compost and the air cool and grow the seedlings on until they are large enough to plant out.

Dryopteris affinis unfurling

Adiantum
Adiantum pedatum (zones 3-8) is hardy and deciduous, producing pinnate mid-green fronds on near-black stems. It spreads by creeping rhizomes to 12 in (30 cm), but is slow to colonize. *A. venustum* (zones 5-8) is evergreen except in very cold winters. The fronds are mid-green on black stems and made up of fan-shaped segments. New growths appear in late winter, bright pink in color. It spreads fairly quickly by rhizomes and grows to 6 in (15 cm)

Asplenium scolopendrium (zones 6-8)
Hart's tongue fern is evergreen with creeping rhizomes and strap-like, leathery, bright green fronds with wavy margins. Height and spread 24 in (60 cm).

Athyrium filix-femina (zones 4-9)
Lady fern loves a moist, slightly acid, shady soil. Deciduous and very hardy, it produces 3 ft (1 m) long, pale green fronds like shuttlecocks in early spring and spreads to 3 ft (1 m). The 'Plumosum Cristatum Group' all have beautifully crested and finely cut fronds.

Onoclea sensibilis

Blechnum

Blechnum penna-marina (zones 10-11) requires a moist acid soil in full shade. It is an evergreen whose sterile and fertile fronds rise separately from the rhizomes. Growing to 8 in (20 cm), it spreads rapidly in a woodland site.

Blechnum spicant (zones 5-8) is evergreen and as the sterile fronds age they become almost horizontal, making excellent ground cover and producing a rosette around the vertical fertile fronds. Forming clumps of 24 in (60 cm) or more, it spreads by rhizomes.

Dryopteris

Dryopteris affinis (golden male fern) (zones 6-8) is a semi-evergreen, the young pale green shuttlecocks appearing in early spring to contrast with the light brown mid-ribs. Height and spread 36 in (90 cm).

The following are all deciduous. *Dryopteris carthusiana* (narrow buckler fern) (zones 6-8) has pale green fronds growing to 24 in (60 cm). It is quite hardy, enjoying boggy soil. *D. erythrosora* (zones 6-9) has coppery fronds turning shiny bright green as they mature. It enjoys a moist, sheltered area, spreading slowly. *D. filix-mas*, known simply as the male fern, (zones 4-8) with a height and spread of 3 ft (1 m), quickly forms a large clump dying down late in the season. The new growths of *D. wallichiana* (zones 7-9) are pale green with black scales and grow to 6 ft (1.8 m).

Gymnocarpium

Gymnocarpium dryopteris (oak fern) (zones 4-8) is deciduous with pale green, triangular fronds appearing in early spring and later turning to a deep green. I'm sure that the paint manufacturers were thinking of the mature leaves when they labelled paint 'fern green'. It will grow to about 8 in (20 cm).

Gymnocarpium robertianum (zones 3-7) is similar to the oak fern but will grow to 16 in (40 cm). It spreads rapidly by rhizomes and makes ideal ground cover in shady, damp sites.

Onoclea sensibilis (zones 4-9)

Hardy, but dislikes a sunny site, where its fronds will scorch. It is deciduous, with pale green, sterile fronds 24 in (60 cm) high in early spring. The ideal site is a damp, shaded area or the edge of a pond or stream, where it will spread rapidly.

Osmunda regalis (zones 4-9)

My all-time favorite fern. The genus *Osmunda* is found in all the continents with the exception of Australasia, which is about the only reason I can think of for not wanting to live in Australia. Commonly called the royal fern, it is deciduous with bright green sterile fronds growing to 36 in (90 cm). The fertile fronds grow longer – to 6 ft 6in (2 m) – and in summer are plastered with brown spores which look like blossom. Osmunda fiber is used as a potting compost for orchids. A good plant will spread to 13 ft (4 m).

Polypodium vulgare (zones 6-8)

Common polypody has dark green, evergreen fronds, growing to 12 in (30 cm) and spreading all over the place. The variety 'Cornubiense' is even more vigorous and is excellent for ground cover.

Polystichum

One of the best genera of evergreen ferns. *Polystichum aculeatum* (hard shield fern) (zones 3-6) has shiny, dark green fronds 24 in (60 cm high) that spread to 36 in (90 cm). *P. setiferum* (soft shield fern) (zones 5-8) has soft, dark green fronds 4 ft (1.2 m) high, while the fronds of *P. munitum* (giant holly fern), (zones 3-8) also dark green, are leathery with spiny margins.

Polystichum munitum

CONIFERS

Not all conifers are evergreen – indeed, some of my favorites are deciduous, including larch (Larix), maidenhair tree (Gingko) and dawn redwood (Metasequoia). However it is the evergreens that are useful for ground cover, with their dense net of scale-like leaves in a whole range of colors from gold through yellow and green variegations, bronze, blue and the proverbial forty shades of green. The plant shape ranges from solid, prostrate sheets of branches and dumpy mounds, through tiers of horizontal branches to fast-growing trees.

Given time, conifers will subdue all but the most persistent of weeds. The junipers give the biggest choice of species and varieties, but some of the yews and spruces are also worth growing. Most garden conifers prefer a light, open, well-drained, acid soil in full sun, although yews will grow in shade and yews and junipers will thrive on lime.

Like all evergreens, conifers are best transplanted when the soil is warm with rain to follow. Autumn and spring are ideal, but if the weather is not harsh they can be planted and moved throughout winter. The plant spacing should be generous as they can cover a lot of ground. If conifers have been planted too close to each other try to thin them out before they overlap, to prevent plants turning brown on the sides that are in competition.

You should be aware of some terms used to describe conifers. There is an enormous difference between a 'slow-growing conifer' and a 'dwarf conifer'. The former may not grow much in a year, but in a lifetime it might grow to a size totally unsuitable for a small garden. The speed with which such plants spread can catch you unawares, swamping less vigorous plants nearby. Labels often state the size the plant will reach after ten years, but it is worth seeking out a knowledgeable member of staff in the garden center and finding out the final size.

Juniperus communis

Juniperus

The junipers are undoubtedly the biggest group of conifers and the best for ground cover.

Juniperus virginiana 'Blue Cloud' (zones 3-9) is a wide-spreading conifer that will eventually grow 5 ft (1.5 m) high. The branches are thin and whippy and glaucous blue all year round.

Juniperus communis (common juniper) (zones 2-6) grows naturally in most of the northern hemisphere. Its round black fruits are used to flavor gin, which is, in itself, a good enough reason to grow it. The prostrate forms of *J. communis* are especially useful for ground covering in full sun. *J. c.* 'Depressa' will spread well, covering 5 ft (1.5 m) and is fairly prostrate, reaching 24 in (60 cm) in height. The pointed leaves are a dull yellow, turning brownish green in winter. One of the best ground-cover plants for a sunny, dry bank. *J. c.* 'Depressa Aurea' is of similar habit but with golden yellow foliage in summer. The variety *J. c.* 'Hornibrookii' used to be called 'Prostrata', which was a much better name because the plant hugs the ground, taking on the shape of any object it grows over. It grows 8 in

Juniperus squamata 'Blue Star' and Erica carnea 'Fox Hollow'

Right *Juniperus communis* 'Repanda'

(20 cm) high, spreading to 6 ft 6 in (2 m). The original plant was found by Murray Hornibrook in Co. Galway, Ireland. It's a pity it wasn't found by Mr Prostrate. 'Repanda' is another carpeter, with softer leaves that turn bronze in winter. It has a similar spread to 'Hornibrookii'.

Juniperus conferta (shore juniper) (zones 5-9) has bright green leaves with a white band on the upper surface. It grows to 12 in (30 cm) high and will spread forever. I have seen plants covering 16 ft (5 m) in a few years. It will enjoy dry sandy soils in full sun.

Juniperus horizontalis (creeping juniper) (zones 3-9) has needle-like juvenile gray-green foliage, hugging the ground and forming a dense carpet only 12 in (30 cm) high but spreading for enormous distances. This is an accommodating plant that can tolerate wet or dry soil conditions. Some of its varieties offer a change in foliage: 'Bar Harbor' has gray-green leaves, 'Blue Chip' is bright blue and 'Emerald Spreader' forms mats of bright green foliage.

Juniperus x *media* 'Pfitzeriana' (zones 4-9) and its sports are the best known of the low-growing conifers and yet are far from prostrate, forming a medium-sized plant with a height and spread of up to 6 ft 6 in (2 m) and tiers of angled branches. Quick-

Microbiota decussata

Juniperus procumbens 'Nana'

growing, the foliage is dull green. The sport *J.* x *m.* 'Pfitzeriana Aurea' has golden yellow foliage turning green in winter.

Juniperus procumbens (zones 5-9) has blue-green foliage and quickly forms dense mats up to 6 ft (2 m) wide and 12 in (30 cm) high. It likes a light, free-draining soil in full sun. The dwarf form *J. p.* 'Nana' is less vigorous, spreading only to 30 in (75 cm). *J. squamata* 'Blue Star' (zones 5-8) forms a low mound, spreading only to 3 ft (1 m), but making up for that with its beautiful silvery blue foliage.

Microbiota decussata (zones 3-7)
The mid-green foliage turns completely brown in winter, so that the plant appears to be dead. Some garden centers won't stock it because customers return it when it 'dies'. The foliage contrasts well with some of the paler green junipers such as *Juniperus conferta*. It likes a well-drained soil and spreads quickly to cover 6 ft 6 in (2 m).

Pinus mugo 'Mops' (zones 3-7)
A slow-growing pine with small, well-spaced, bright green leaves. It eventually produces dark brown female cones. Height 10 ft (3 m), spread 16 ft (5 m).

Podocarpus alpinus (zones 7-10)
Grows to 6 ft 6 in (2 m) in height and spread, with densely packed branches of gray-green leaves. Female plants produce shiny red fruit. A good plant for stony sites or scree beds.

Taxus (zones 7-8)
Taxus baccata 'Repandens' is a female yew that doesn't produce any leaders but spreads by side shoots, forming a low mound extending to over 16 ft (5 m) and 24 in (60 cm) high. It will tolerate full sun or partial shade. *T. b.* 'Repens Aurea' has leaves edged gold on young growths, turning pale cream later in summer and spreading to 6 ft 6 in (2 m). *T. b.* 'Summergold' I like because it spreads quickly, forming a low carpeting conifer, but with enough height to show off its bright golden yellow foliage. In winter it reverts to green-margined yellow.

Tsuga canadensis 'Prostrata' (zones 4-8)
Flat-growing with dull green foliage and its branches tight to the ground. The stems spread in all directions, slowly forming large mats. If you are not in a hurry it will make excellent ground cover.

GRASSES

Some of the ornamental grasses can work in the same way as ferns. Their narrow leaves and, in some cases, their height act as a foil for broader-leaved shrubs. Some of the flowers are spectacular. Some of the Stipa flower at 6 ft (1.8 m) with golden, plumy heads. Other grasses, including the fescues, have variegated or blue foliage forming dense mats of color. As a front to bolder green or yellow-leaved plants they make an effective display in summer.

Some species are troublesome, seeding as if their lives depended upon it and not having the decency to come true to their parents. A notable exception is Bowles' golden grass (Milium effusum 'Aureum'), which is pale sulphur yellow in spring and comes true from seed. Some grasses are useful, helping to bind fine soils and prevent wind erosion. But many are simply ornamental and ideal as a means of controlling weeds without taking over the weeds' role.

All the grasses listed here are perennials, the deciduous species reappearing early in spring.

Carex

Carex comans (zones 7-9) is a sedge from New Zealand, hardy in all but the coldest areas. It is a tufted evergreen that dislikes wet soils. The foliage color is variable from reddish brown to pale yellow-green. Each tuft will grow to 10 in (25 cm) and spread reasonably quickly to 30 in (75 cm). *C. elata* 'Aurea' (Bowles' golden sedge) (zones 5-9) is deciduous, spreading by rhizomes and enjoying damp conditions in a sunny or partially shaded site. The long, narrow and arching golden leaves are edged with pale green. Grows to 30 in (75 cm) with a spread of 18 in (45 cm).

Carex hachijoensis 'Evergold' (zones 6-9) is a lovely evergreen sedge, spreading by rhizomes. The dark green leaves have a wide, central, creamy yellow stripe and do best in a rich moist soil. Height and spread 12 in (30 cm).

Carex pendula (weeping sedge) (zones 5-9) is a beautiful, big brute, evergreen and growing nearly 6 ft (2 m) tall with a spread of 5 ft (1.5 m). The shiny green leaves are surpassed by long, arching stems of flowers with dark brown, catkin-like 6 in (15 cm) long spikes in late spring and early summer.

Carex siderosticha 'Variegata' (zones 6-9) is deciduous, spreading slowly to 18 in (45 cm). It is low-growing, reaching 12 in (30 cm). The pale green leaves are broad with a white margin and stripes, while the base of the plant is marked with pink.

Festuca

Festuca eskia's (zones 5-7) deep green leaves will form a carpet in time. Each plant grows to 6 in (15 cm) high with a spread of 12 in (30 cm). *F. glauca* (zones 4-8) is an attractive tufted evergreen with inrolled, smooth, blue-green leaves. 'Blue Fox' has bright blue leaves. Height and spread 12 in (30 cm).

Glyceria maxima (zones 5-9)

Once you have got this you can't get rid of it! Ideal for the margins of large ponds where it can be contained in a pot, it will grow in any moist soil. The leaves are deep green but the form 'Variegata' is more interesting with its white, cream and green foliage. Both will grow to 36 in (90 cm) high and will spread quickly to cover large areas. To keep my clump within bounds I divide it in half every two years. The only weed that has ever managed to establish itself inside the clump is a bramble.

Luzula

Luzula nivea (woodrush) (zones 4-9) is evergreen with deep green leaves and panicles of bright white flowers in summer. The flower heads can be dried. Grows to 24 in (60 cm) high and slowly spreads to 18 in (45 cm).

Luzula sylvatica (greater woodrush) (zones 5-9) is very hardy with dark green leaves. Brown panicles of flowers are produced in late spring. Grows to 30 in (75 cm) tall and will spread 18 in (45 cm), forming good ground cover. *L. s.* 'Aurea' has bright, shiny, golden yellow leaves in winter, turning paler yellow in summer.

Milium effusum 'Aureum' (zones 5-9)

Bowles' golden grass is a great wee semi-evergreen, producing, in spring, rich, soft yellow leaves that pale as the season advances. In summer thin, golden-stemmed panicles appear. Grows to 24 in (60 cm) high and spreads to 12 in (30 cm).

Phalaris arundinacea (zones 4-9)

Ribbon grass is a weed and that is my honest opinion. Having said that I have several clumps of it and the variegated *P. a.* 'Picta', (gardeners' garters) and am very glad of them. 'Picta' has white-striped leaves and *P. a.* 'Feesey' has broad, creamy striped leaves. All grow to 3 ft (1 m) and spread as far as you will allow them.

Stipa gigantea (zones 7-10)

Golden oats is a graceful, clump-forming evergreen with mid-green leaves. The 6 ft 6 in (2 m) high silver-purple spikelets turn yellow when ripe and are carried like stalks of oats. It will cover 3 ft (1 m).

Phalaris arundinacea 'Picta'

HEATHERS

The three genera that make up this group – Erica, Calluna *and* Daboecia *– are invaluable as dense, low-growing coverers. They all spread quickly, knitting into each other and forming mats of color seldom more than 20-24 in (50-60 cm) high. They anchor the soil and the surface roots deter all but the strongest weeds. With careful choice it is possible to have color all year round. Where I live,* Erica cinerea *flowers in June, followed by* E. vagans. Calluna vulgaris *stays in flower until early November, and is followed by* E. x darleyensis *and then* E. carnea, *taking me through until the end of April.*

Calluna species need a lime-free soil rich in humus and enjoy an open exposed site with the wind in their hair. *Erica* is not so fussy, E. carnea, E. x darleyensis *and* E. mediterranea *tolerating some lime in the soil. They dislike growing under trees, preferring an open site in full sun and a light soil.* Daboecia *dislikes lime and does best in a rich, well-drained soil.*

Pruning is necessary to stop the plants becoming leggy. Clip off most or all of the dead flower stems to allow new shoots to form low down the stems. Try to prevent leaves lying on the foliage in autumn, brushing or blowing them off if necessary. Older plants will enjoy a mulch of rotted compost or peat washed down around the base of the stems.

Erica x darleyensis 'Darley Dale'

Left *Glyceria maxima* with *Crocosmia* in the background

Calluna vulgaris (zones 4-7)

Commonly known as heather or ling. There is an enormous range of varieties of *Calluna*, in a wonderful selection of colors, with different growth habits and flowers at various times from midsummer to midwinter. All demand a lime-free soil and prefer an open, sunny site, but can tolerate some shade. New varieties are appearing on the market at an incredible rate but this selection has stood or will stand the test of time.

C. v. 'Alba Rigida' has white flowers in late summer on stems that are almost horizontal. Grows to only 6 in (15 cm) high. 'County Wicklow' is, like the county itself, enjoyable and charming, flowering from late summer into autumn. The pale pink flowers are fully double and produced freely. Growing to 10 in (25 cm) it forms a dwarf, bushy, spreading plant. 'Golden Carpet' I would grow mainly for its foliage, which is bright orange-yellow and forms a low carpet of color. In summer deep pink flowers are produced. 'Hibernica' is extremely low-growing, reaching only 6 in (15 cm) and flowering from late autumn well into winter. The mauve blooms plaster the plant, completely covering the foliage. 'Mrs Ronald Grey' has to be seen to be believed. It forms a prostrate carpet, reaching only 3 in (7 cm) high and hugging the shape of everything it covers. The purple-red flowers are carried on tiny stems during late summer.

Frosted foliage on *Erica carnea* 'Springwood Pink'

Daboecia cantabrica (zones 6-8)

Connemara heath loves a well-drained, acid soil in full sun and flowers over a long period from early summer through to mid-winter. It will grow to 18 in (45 cm) tall with a spread of 24 in (60 cm). As plants get older they tend to become straggly and benefit from a light pruning in early spring. *D. cantabrica* itself is rose-purple but colors of other varieties range from white through pink to deep red and purple. Good varieties include : 'Alba', with white flowers; 'Bicolor', which has white, striped and rose-colored flowers on the same stem; 'Praegerae', which is slightly different with narrow, deep pink flowers on a dwarf plant that tends to spread.

Erica carnea (zones 5-7)

This is a great heather, not least because it can tolerate lime in the soil. Low-growing, it will quickly form a carpet of easily maintained growth. The species plant produces rosy red flowers throughout the winter months, but

Erica vagans

Erica cinerea (bell heather) (zones 6-8) is well known as the wild purple heather found on British moorlands. It is summer-flowering and grows to 10 in (25 cm), slowly forming a carpet of tough, wiry stems. The variety 'Alba Minor' is white flowering and grows only to 6 in (15 cm). 'C. D. Eason' spreads to 20 in (50 cm) with deep pink flowers all summer. The foliage of 'Fiddler's Gold' is yellow and red-tinted when young, turning to pale green; the flowers are purple. It quickly spreads to 20 in (50 cm).

Erica x *darleyensis* (zones 7-8) is a useful heather in that it and its varieties are tolerant of lime and grow to about 20 in (50 cm) high. Winter-flowering, they combine well with *Erica carnea*. 'Darley Dale' is the best known variety, forming a clump of pale pink flowers. 'Furzey' has dark green foliage and deep pink flowers for most of the winter. 'Silberschmelze' has scented white flowers and carries its blooms all winter, but it is not a good spreader.

Erica erigena (zones 8-9) is lime-tolerant, flowering in spring with a show of perfumed, rosy red flowers. It grows to a majestic 6 ft 6 in (2 m) with a spread of 36 in (90 cm), although some of its varieties are not so vigorous. 'Golden Lady' is more compact, reaching 12 in (30 cm) in height with golden yellow foliage and white flowers.

Erica tetralix (cross-leaved heath) (zones 5-7) flowers from summer through autumn with deep pink blooms and is low-growing to about 20 in (50 cm). 'L. E. Underwood' forms silvery gray mounds with light pink flowers. 'Pink Star' has gray-green foliage, lilac-pink blooms and is low-growing, forming a pretty pink carpet in summer.

Erica vagans (Cornish heath) (zones 7-9) is a spreader that flowers in late summer. The variety 'Cream' has white flowers on light green foliage. 'Mrs D. F. Maxwell' grows to 20 in (50 cm) with deep cerise flowers.

within its cultivars there are whites, pinks and purples, flowering from early winter to late spring. 'Ann Sparkes' flowers in spring, with golden foliage and purple flowers. It spreads slowly to form good cover 8 in (20 cm) high. 'Eileen Porter' is one of my favorites. It is low-growing, flowering from late autumn until spring with carmine red flowers. The calyces are pale pink, producing a bicolor effect. 'March Seedling' is another low-growing spreader with pale purple flowers and deep green foliage. 'Springwood White' is a lovely ground-covering plant with a spread of 24 in (60 cm) and masses of large white flowers making their display in the dead of winter. 'Springwood Pink' is the same as its sister (heather must be female!) but with clear rose-pink flowers. The two combine well. 'Vivellii' is a favorite winter-flowering variety with brilliant deep red blooms and bronzy purple foliage in winter, making about 10 in (25 cm) in height.

Erica ciliaris (Dorset heath) (zones 8-9) flowers from the height of summer until autumn with largish rosy red blooms. All varieties are fairly low-growing – to 8 in (20 cm) – and spread quite quickly to 24 in (60 cm). 'Corfe Castle' has pale pink flowers and the leaves turn bronze in winter. 'David McClintock' is unusual, having white flowers tipped with clear pink and gray foliage. It was found by David in Brittany.

■ **RIGHT** Many common herbs enjoy similar conditions, so you can happily grow sage, mint and thyme in the same bed. Beware of the mint's tendency to take over, though.

HERBS

I was once asked, 'Are all plants herbs?' and while the short answer is no, an awful lot of them are. Herbs overlap with lots of other groups of plants. Lavender is a herb, but also a useful shrub in its own right. Lady's mantle is a medicinal herb that doubles up as a lovely herbaceous perennial. So plants that are best known for their herbal qualities will be listed in this section and cross-referenced under other headings. Since this is a book on plants suitable for ground cover, I do not intend, nor am I qualified, to extol the virtues of herbs in regard to their suitability for culinary, medicinal, cosmetic or indeed witchcraft uses.

Some trees and shrubs can be considered as herbs, but what annoys me is the undeniable fact that weeds are considered herbs. I refuse to grow nettles and ground elder in the herb garden, but lots of weeds have great pedigrees. Take ground elder, for example. Aegopodium podagraria *has been with us since the Middle Ages. The generic name is supposed to be from the Greek,* aigos *for goat and* podos *for foot, the idea being that the leaf looks (vaguely) like a goat's foot. The specific name is from the Latin* podagra *meaning gout, as the plant has, for centuries, been used to treat gout – hence the common name of gout weed. St Gerard is the patron saint of gout sufferers, so we get Herb Gerard. The other common nickname, bishops weed, may be intended to stop you swearing at it as it covers your garden, but it is more likely to be because it was grown in monasteries as a medicinal herb. It has survived on many sites where the monasteries didn't.*

Dense plantings of shrubs such as rosemary and lavender will certainly inhibit weeds. Bay grown as a shrub and, at the other end of the scale, thyme grown as a carpet will be equally successful. Traditionally many herbs are grown in poor, thin soils with only a little added nutrient to enhance the flavor or the perfume; these same conditions will deter weeds. Herbs used in large groupings can look forlorn in winter and are more likely to gladden the eye if mixed with less straggly company. Plants such as lavender, curry plant and catmint will benefit from being pruned after flowering or in early spring to keep them compact. Cut the flowering stems back to within 2 in (5 cm) of the previous year's growth.

Calamintha nepeta (zones 5-9)
Calamint is a perennial with peppermint-scented leaves and pink, lilac or white flowers in summer. *C. grandiflora* 'Variegata' has large, bright pink flowers and variegated leaves. Both grow to 18 in (45 cm) with a spread of 36 in (90 cm).

Chamaemelum nobile (zones 6-9)
Roman chamomile takes its name from the Greek *chamaimelon*, which translates as 'the apple on the ground' and refers to the scent of apples released when the plant is trodden on. It is a carpet-forming, evergreen perennial producing small, long-

Calamintha nepeta 'White Cloud'

stalked, daisy-like white flowers with yellow centers in summer. It grows to 6 in (15 cm) high with a spread of 18 in (45 cm).

Chamaemelum nobile 'Treneague' is non-flowering, growing only 1 in (3 cm) high and is the ideal choice for a lawn. But unless your heart is absolutely set on a chamomile lawn, don't go to the trouble. Usually it ends up patchy with bald areas and lots of weeds. You are afraid to walk on it as it cannot stand the abuse, so you don't get the scent from the crushed foliage.

Galium odoratum

Galium odoratum (zones 5-8)
Woodruff is a deciduous perennial with lanceolate leaves and star-shaped, fragrant, white flowers in early summer. It makes good summer ground cover in a shaded site. Height 18 in (45 cm) and will spread far and wide.

Helichrysum italicum (zones 7-10)
Curry plant is a dense evergreen shrub with silvery leaves and small orange-yellow flowers that are on show all summer. The whole plant smells of curry and it seems stronger after a shower of rain. If, like me, you dislike curry, don't grow this plant. Height 24 in (60 cm), spread 36 in (90 cm).

Hyssopus officinalis (zones 6-9)
Hyssop is a semi-evergreen perennial with pale green leaves and purple flowers in late summer. Growing to 24 in (60 cm) high and

spreading to 36 in (90 cm), it likes a poor, dry sandy soil. *H. o.* 'Albus' is an excellent white form.

Lavandula
Lavandula angustifolia (lavender or English lavender) (zones 5-8) is an ideal dwarf hedge. It is summer-flowering and evergreen, with downy white leaves that later turn green, and aromatic, purple flowers on long stalks. Height and spread 36 in (90 cm). There are many varieties including 'Munstead', early-flowering with bright lavender-blue flowers and 'Hidcote' with deep violet flowers

Lavandula dentata (fringed leaved lavender) (zones 8-9) has toothed, gray-green leaves, woolly on the underside, and dense spikes of deep blue flowers in late summer. Height and spread 24 in (60 cm).

Lavandula stoechas (French or Spanish lavender) (zones 8-9) forms a dense, bushy shrub with light green leaves and a height and spread of 24 in (60 cm). The rather long spikes of purple flowers are topped with two purple bracts. *L. s. leucantha* is a white-flowering form.

Mentha
More popularly known as mint, and that one word can have gardeners quaking in their welly boots and shouting for a bucket to grow it in to contain its spread. There is no arguing with any fantastic claims about its travelling capabilities – most reference books only quote its height and put its spread down as indefinite.

Mentha x *gracilis* (gingermint) (zones 6-9) is a perennial with smooth leaves and a sweet smell. The flowers are mauve in separated whorls up the stem. Grows to 24 in (60 cm). *M.* x *g.* 'Variegata' has green leaves blotched with pale yellow and grows to the same height, producing a fruity fragrance

Mentha longifolia (horse mint) (zones 6-9) has peppermint-scented gray-green leaves brightened by long spikes of flowers, like a miniature buddleia, in mauve, pink or white. It can grow to 3 ft (1 m) high.

Ruta graveolens 'Jackmans Blue'

Mentha x *piperita* 'Citrata' (eau-de-cologne mint or lemon mint) (zones 3-7) has rounded, bronze-green leaves and smells of lavender. Pale pink whorls of bloom stretch up the stems. Height 18 in (45 cm).

Mentha pulegium (pennyroyal) (zones 7-9) is a real ground coverer, creeping in every direction with small, pungent leaves and pale purple flowers, growing to 6 in (15 cm) high. The variety 'Cunningham Mint' is lower, growing only 4 in (10 cm) high.

Mentha requienii (Corsican mint) (zones 6-9) carpets the ground, the stems rooting as they spread. The minute leaves smell unpleasant. Small pink flowers appear in summer. 2 in (5 cm) is about the maximum height.

Mentha spicata (spearmint) (zones 3-7) has bright green, crinkled leaves with a sweet scent. The flowers can be white, pink or lilac in long spikes and can grow to 3 ft (1 m) high.

Mentha suaveolens 'Variegata' (pineapple mint) (zones 6-9). My favorite mint (for looking at) with creamy white variegation and quite often whole stems and leaves totally white. It has a pleasant fruity smell. It is of variable height but can grow to 3 ft (1 m).

Nepeta cataria (zones 3-7)
Catnip or catmint owes its name to the effect it has on cats, which eat it and roll in it with total abandon. It has small, gray-green leaves with white and purple flowers in summer and early autumn. Height and

spread 24 in (60 cm). There is another catmint, *Nepeta* x *faassenii*, that is not a herb but is useful for ground cover. See **Herbaceous Plants**, page 127.

Origanum

Origanum dictamnus (hop marjoram) (zones 8-10) is a flat-growing sub-shrub with rounded, woolly, silvery white leaves. The pink summer flowers are surrounded by deep red bracts. Height 6 in (15 cm), spread 18 in (45 cm).

Origanum majorana (sweet marjoram) (zones 6-9) is a perennial shrub with gray-green leaves and small pink white flowers in late summer. Height and spread 24 in (60 cm).

Origanum onites (pot marjoram) (zones 8-10) is a perennial with dull green leaves; white or pink clusters of flowers appear in late summer. Height and spread 24 in (60 cm).

Origanum vulgare 'Aureum' (golden marjoram) (zones 5-9) has yellowish green leaves and purple flowers, but requires some shade as the foliage scorches in full sun. Height and spread 24 in (60 cm).

Plantago asiatica 'Variegata' (zones 7-8)

Remember that plantains are troublesome weeds of lawns and hard surfaces and treat them with a degree of caution. This variety has white splashes over the leaves, making it just about worth growing. Height 10 in (25 cm) spread 12 in (30 cm).

Rosmarinus (zones 7-9)

Rosemary is an aromatic, evergreen shrub with stiff, upright branches and thin green leaves. The flowers appear in spring in shades from palest pinky blue to deep royal blue. Height and spread 6 ft 6 in (2 m). *Rosmarinus officinalis albiflorus* has white flowers; *R. o.* 'Aureus' has leaves with a yellow variegation and pale blue flowers. The variety 'McConnell's Blue' is a prostrate plant and a good ground-coverer with lots of mid-blue flowers. Height 12 in (30 cm) spread 3 ft (90 cm). 'Miss Jessopp's Upright' is a useful, upright-growing shrub for the herb border or for dry stony sites. It produces masses of pale blue flowers and reaches 6 ft 6 in (2 m) in height and spread.

The Prostratus Group is low-growing, covering the allotted space quickly with grayish green leaves and pale blue flowers. Height 12 in (30 cm), spread 3 ft (90 cm)

Ruta graveolens (zones 5-9)

Rue is an evergreen shrub with deeply cut, dark green leaves and deep yellow summer flowers. The foliage could be described as strong smelling, but should be described as horrible smelling, and care should be taken not to touch the foliage as it can cause the skin rash photodermatitis. Height 24 in (60 cm), spread 18 in (45 cm). The variety *Ruta graveolens* 'Jackman's Blue' has deep blue-gray leaves. *R. g.* 'Variegata' is quite attractive, with creamy white leaf markings, and will come true from seed. Both varieties have the same erect habit as *R. graveolens*.

Teucrium

Teucrium chamaedrys (germander) (zones 5-9) is useful for steep banks. A small, evergreen spreader, it has shiny, green, aromatic leaves and deep pink blooms all summer and autumn. Height and spread 6 in (15 cm). *T. divaricatum* (zones 7-9) is more upright, growing to 30 in (75 cm) and makes a good hedging plant for use in knot gardens.

Thymus

Everyone knows thyme, its aroma is recognised and it would be hard to find anything in the plant to complain about. It spreads well, rooting as it goes, but without being invasive. There are over 350 species and practically all of them flower profusely, producing copious amounts of nectar for the making of honey. They tolerate dry, stony, infertile soils and are quite hardy.

Thymus x *citriodorus* (lemon thyme) (zones 6-9) has lemon-scented foliage with pale lilac flowers in summer. Height 12 in (30 cm), spread 24 in (60 cm). In the variety 'Bertram Anderson' the new growth is tinged with red, turning golden later. It grows only to 6 in (15 cm), spreading to 24 in (60 cm). 'Silver Queen' has variegated leaves with either silver or gold markings and a strong lemon scent. Height 8 in (20 cm), spread 12 in (30 cm).

Thymus serpyllum (wild thyme or mother of thyme) (zones 4-9) is prostrate in habit, with small hairy leaves and light purple flowers all summer. Height 2 in (5 cm), spread 36 in (90 cm). The variety 'Pink Chintz' has pale green leaves and masses of pale pink flowers. It is vigorous, very low-growing at 2 in (5 cm) and spreads to 24 in (60 cm).

Thymus vulgaris (common thyme) (zones 4-9) will grow to 18 in (45 cm) and spread to 24 in (60 cm). It has gray-green leaves and flower color from purple through to pale pink. *T. v.* 'Silver Posie' is a real wee beauty with tiny, white-variegated leaves and masses of pink-purple flowers. Height 12 in (30 cm), spread 18 in (45 cm).

Viola

Viola odorata (sweet violet) (zones 7-9) is a perennial spreading by stolons and has white or purple, deliciously sweet-smelling flowers. The cut flowers used to be sold in small bunches, but I haven't seen any for ages. *V. o.* 'Alba' has pure white flowers and both grow to a height of 6 in (15 cm) and spread of 12 in (30 cm).

Viola tricolor (heartsease, wild pansy) (zones 4-8) is a small, slender, short-lived perennial with pansy-like blooms of mixed colors of yellow, white and purple in summer. Height and spread 12 in (30 cm).

Viola tricolor

BULBS, CORMS, RHIZOMES AND TUBERS

Some of these are extremely useful ground-coverers. They are mostly deciduous, although in mild climates some will remain in leaf. One part of my garden is very sheltered and the clumps of arum lily growing there never lose their leaves, whereas in a draughty cold part they die down every winter, reappearing in spring. The spread noted here reflects the growth of an individual plant, although many will multiply, colonizing rapidly and forming solid areas of plants.

Anemone

Anemone apennina (zones 6-9) is a perennial with creeping rhizomes and dark green leaves. The spring flowers are usually bright blue, occasionally white or pale pink. Height 8 in (20 cm), spread 12 in (30 cm).

Anemone blanda (zones 4-8) is a spreading perennial with irregular tubers and dark green leaves. In spring the flowers are produced above the leaves. Named varieties include 'Radar' (deep magenta with a white center), 'Violet Star' (purple with a white center), 'Atrocaerulea' (deep blue) and 'Charmer' (pink). Height and spread 6 in (15 cm). *A. nemerosa* (wood anemone) (zones 4-8) is low-growing, spreading by rhizome, with pale green leaves and single white flowers in spring. Height 6 in (15 cm), spread 12 in (30 cm).

Arum creticum

Arisaema sikokianum (zones 5-9)

Tuberous perennial with dark green leaves, usually three- and five-lobed, producing a long, brown-purple spathe in spring. The white, stunted and club-like spadix is clearly visible in the base. Likes a sheltered site. Height 20 in (50 cm), spread 6 in (15 cm).

Arisarum proboscideum (zones 7-9)

Dense, spreading, rhizomatous perennial with shiny, dark green, arrow-shaped leaves. Flowers appear in spring and are often hidden by the foliage. Small hooded spathes have long thin tips, deep brown fading to white at the base. Height 6 in (15 cm), spread 12 in (30 cm).

Arum creticum (zones 8-10)

Lords and ladies are tuberous perennials with dark green, arrow-shaped leaves and deep yellow spathes in spring. They curve out at the tip, revealing a yellow and fragrant spadix. Height 18 in (45 cm), spread 8 in (20 cm).

Convallaria majalis (zones 2-7)

Lily of the valley is a rhizomatous perennial with pairs of shiny, mid-green, basal leaves and bell-shaped, waxy, white, heavily scented flowers on arching stems in late spring. Spreads rapidly to colonise large areas. Height and spread 10 in (25 cm). The variety *C. m.* 'Albostriata' has creamy white stripes on the leaves. *C. m.* 'Rosea' has lilac-pink flowers.

Crocosmia (zones 6-9)

Crocosmia 'Lucifer' is a strong-growing perennial from a corm, with sword-like, mid-green, ribbed leaves and long-stemmed spikes of upward-pointing clear red flowers in summer. Height 36 in (90 cm), spread 4 in (10 cm) but will quickly colonize a larger area. *C.* 'Solfatare'

Arisaena sikokianum

rapidly forms large clumps. It has bronze-green leaves and orange-yellow flowers in summer. Height 24 in (60 cm), spread 4 in (10 cm).

Cyclamen (zones 5-9)

Cyclamen cilicium is a tuberous perennial whose rounded, mid-green leaves have pale green patterns. The flowers are white or pink with a deep red stain at the mouth. A pure white form, *C. c.* 'Album', flowers in late summer and autumn, the leaves appear at the same time. Height 2 in (5 cm), spread 4 in (10 cm). *C. coum* has rounded, dark green leaves, often mottled with silver, appearing in winter and early spring with the deep pink, shuttlecock flowers. Height and spread 4 in (10 cm). *C. hederifolium* has ivy-shaped leaves mottled light and dark green with silver markings. The flowers appear just before the leaves in early to mid-winter and are icing-sugar pink with darker pink towards the mouth. Height and spread 6 in (15 cm).

Dahlia (zones 8-9)

Tuberous, half-hardy perennial, usually bushy, with good leaf cover. Can be grown

Right *Cyclamen coum*

Hyacinthoides hispanica

from the fleshy tubers, planted outdoors once the risk of frost is past, or from seed, to flower in the same year. There are 11 dahlia groups, based on flower shape, e.g. cactus, pompon and decorative. Leaves can be dull or glossy, pale, mid-or dark green on thick, pale green stems. Flowers are produced during summer and autumn in a range of colors from purest white to deepest red. Height ranges from the dwarf bedding at 6 in (15 cm) to 5 ft (1.5 m), with a spread of 12–24 in (30–60 cm).

Eranthis hyemalis (zones 4-9)
Winter aconite is a perennial with knobbly tubers and bright green circles of leaves below large, bright yellow flowers in late winter and early spring. Spreads quickly to form large clumps. Height and spread 2 in (5 cm).

Erythronium dens-canis (zones 3-9)
Dog's-tooth violet is a bulbous perennial with mid-green leaves heavily marked with purplish brown. White, pink or lilac flowers appear in spring. Height and spread 6 in (15 cm).

Fritillaria imperialis (zones 5-9)
Crown imperial is a bulbous perennial with

pale green leaves and umbels of bell-shaped flowers in late spring. The heads of 4–8 red, orange or yellow flowers are carried on long stems, have a strong foxy odor and are topped with a cluster of green bracts. Height 4 ft (1.2 m), spread 12 in (30 cm).

Galanthus nivalis (zones 3-9)
The common snowdrop is a bulbous perennial with narrow glaucous leaves and white flowers in winter. The inner tepals have an inverted V-shaped green tip and are slightly fragrant. Height and spread 4 in (10 cm).

Hyacinthoides (zones 4-9)
Hyacinthoides hispanica (Spanish bluebell) is a bulbous perennial with erect, strap-shaped, shiny, dark green leaves and bell-shaped blue flowers on long stalks in spring. *H. h.* 'Excelsior' has violet-blue flowers with a pale blue stripe. Height 20 in (50 cm), spread 4 in (10 cm). Quite rampant, quickly forming large drifts.

Hyacinthoides non-scripta (English bluebell) has long, glossy, dark green leaves and thin, bell-shaped bright blue (sometimes white), scented flowers in spring. The flower stem or raceme is one-sided and droops over at the tip. Height 12 in (30 cm), spread 4 in (10 cm), quickly spreading to cover large areas.

Oxalis
Oxalis adenophylla (zones 6-8) is a bulbous, clump-forming perennial with gray-green, heart-shaped leaves. In spring it produces funnel-shaped, deep pink, purple-veined flowers. Height 4 in (10 cm), spread 6 in (15 cm). *O. enneaphylla* (zones 6-9), a rhizomatous perennial with hairy, pleated, blue-gray leaves, flowers from spring to early summer in a range of shades from white to deep red. Height 4 in (10 cm), spread 6 in (15 cm).

Oxalis oregana (zones 7-9) is a rhizomatous, spreading perennial with hairy, mid-green leaves divided into heart-shaped leaflets. Flowers are produced from spring through to autumn in shades of white, pink or purple. Height 10 in (25 cm), spread indefinite.

Oxalis tetraphylla (good luck plant) (zones 8-9) is a bulbous perennial with leaves

resembling a four-
common name), wi
base of each leaflet.
with yellow center
summer. Height an

Polygonatum
Polygonatum hirt
rhizomatous peren
mid-green leaves.
from the leaf axils fr
summer and are crea
In autumn round
Height 4 ft (1.2 m),
Polygonatum x h
(zones 6-9) is a rh
alternate lance-shap
green-tipped cream
spring, with round
Height 5 ft (1.5 m),

Trillium
Trillium cuneatum
forming, rhizomat
leaves with pale gre
maroon flowers with
sepals smelling of
Height 18 in (45 cm
Trillium grandiflo
5-8) has long, dark
summer it produce
fade to pink, with
above the leaves
18 in (45 cm). *T. g*
double-flowered var
Trillium luteum
mid-green leaves
Deep yellow, sweetl
green sepals are pro
in spring. Height ar

Zantedeschia aethi
Arum lily is a c
from rhizomes,
shaped, shiny gree
in mild locations.
from early to mid-
pure white, each
Height 36 in (90 c

spread 24 in (60 cm). There is another catmint, *Nepeta* x *faassenii*, that is not a herb but is useful for ground cover. See **Herbaceous Plants**, page 127.

Origanum

Origanum dictamnus (hop marjoram) (zones 8-10) is a flat-growing sub-shrub with rounded, woolly, silvery white leaves. The pink summer flowers are surrounded by deep red bracts. Height 6 in (15 cm), spread 18 in (45 cm).

Origanum majorana (sweet marjoram) (zones 6-9) is a perennial shrub with gray-green leaves and small pink white flowers in late summer. Height and spread 24 in (60 cm).

Origanum onites (pot marjoram) (zones 8-10) is a perennial with dull green leaves; white or pink clusters of flowers appear in late summer. Height and spread 24 in (60 cm).

Origanum vulgare 'Aureum' (golden marjoram) (zones 5-9) has yellowish green leaves and purple flowers, but requires some shade as the foliage scorches in full sun. Height and spread 24 in (60 cm).

Plantago asiatica 'Variegata' (zones 7-8)

Remember that plantains are troublesome weeds of lawns and hard surfaces and treat them with a degree of caution. This variety has white splashes over the leaves, making it just about worth growing. Height 10 in (25 cm) spread 12 in (30 cm).

Rosmarinus (zones 7-9)

Rosemary is an aromatic, evergreen shrub with stiff, upright branches and thin green leaves. The flowers appear in spring in shades from palest pinky blue to deep royal blue. Height and spread 6 ft 6 in (2 m). *Rosmarinus officinalis albiflorus* has white flowers; *R. o.* 'Aureus' has leaves with a yellow variegation and pale blue flowers. The variety 'McConnell's Blue' is a prostrate plant and a good ground-coverer with lots of mid-blue flowers. Height 12 in (30 cm) spread 3 ft (90 cm). 'Miss Jessopp's Upright' is a useful, upright-growing shrub for the herb border or for dry stony sites. It produces masses of pale blue flowers and reaches 6 ft 6 in (2 m) in height and spread.

The Prostratus Group is low-growing, covering the allotted space quickly with grayish green leaves and pale blue flowers. Height 12 in (30 cm), spread 3 ft (90 cm)

Ruta graveolens (zones 5-9)

Rue is an evergreen shrub with deeply cut, dark green leaves and deep yellow summer flowers. The foliage could be described as strong smelling, but should be described as horrible smelling, and care should be taken not to touch the foliage as it can cause the skin rash photodermatitis. Height 24 in (60 cm), spread 18 in (45 cm). The variety *Ruta graveolens* 'Jackman's Blue' has deep blue-gray leaves. *R. g.* 'Variegata' is quite attractive, with creamy white leaf markings, and will come true from seed. Both varieties have the same erect habit as *R. graveolens*.

Teucrium

Teucrium chamaedrys (germander) (zones 5-9) is useful for steep banks. A small, evergreen spreader, it has shiny, green, aromatic leaves and deep pink blooms all summer and autumn. Height and spread 6 in (15 cm). *T. divaricatum* (zones 7-9) is more upright, growing to 30 in (75 cm) and makes a good hedging plant for use in knot gardens.

Thymus

Everyone knows thyme, its aroma is recognised and it would be hard to find anything in the plant to complain about. It spreads well, rooting as it goes, but without being invasive. There are over 350 species and practically all of them flower profusely, producing copious amounts of nectar for the making of honey. They tolerate dry, stony, infertile soils and are quite hardy.

Thymus x *citriodorus* (lemon thyme) (zones 6-9) has lemon-scented foliage with pale lilac flowers in summer. Height 12 in (30 cm), spread 24 in (60 cm). In the variety 'Bertram Anderson' the new growth is tinged with red, turning golden later. It grows only to 6 in (15 cm), spreading to 24 in (60 cm). 'Silver Queen' has variegated leaves with either silver or gold markings and a strong lemon scent. Height 8 in (20 cm), spread 12 in (30 cm).

Thymus serpyllum (wild thyme or mother of thyme) (zones 4-9) is prostrate in habit, with small hairy leaves and light purple flowers all summer. Height 2 in (5 cm), spread 36 in (90 cm). The variety 'Pink Chintz' has pale green leaves and masses of pale pink flowers. It is vigorous, very low-growing at 2 in (5 cm) and spreads to 24 in (60 cm).

Thymus vulgaris (common thyme) (zones 4-9) will grow to 18 in (45 cm) and spread to 24 in (60 cm). It has gray-green leaves and flower color from purple through to pale pink. *T. v.* 'Silver Posie' is a real wee beauty with tiny, white-variegated leaves and masses of pink-purple flowers. Height 12 in (30 cm), spread 18 in (45 cm).

Viola

Viola odorata (sweet violet) (zones 7-9) is a perennial spreading by stolons and has white or purple, deliciously sweet-smelling flowers. The cut flowers used to be sold in small bunches, but I haven't seen any for ages. *V. o.* 'Alba' has pure white flowers and both grow to a height of 6 in (15 cm) and spread of 12 in (30 cm).

Viola tricolor (heartsease, wild pansy) (zones 4-8) is a small, slender, short-lived perennial with pansy-like blooms of mixed colors of yellow, white and purple in summer. Height and spread 12 in (30 cm).

Viola tricolor

BULBS, CORMS, RHIZOMES AND TUBERS

Some of these are extremely useful ground-coverers. They are mostly deciduous, although in mild climates some will remain in leaf. One part of my garden is very sheltered and the clumps of arum lily growing there never lose their leaves, whereas in a draughty cold part they die down every winter, reappearing in spring. The spread noted here reflects the growth of an individual plant, although many will multiply, colonizing rapidly and forming solid areas of plants.

Arisaena sikokianum

Anemone

Anemone apennina (zones 6-9) is a perennial with creeping rhizomes and dark green leaves. The spring flowers are usually bright blue, occasionally white or pale pink. Height 8 in (20 cm), spread 12 in (30 cm).

Anemone blanda (zones 4-8) is a spreading perennial with irregular tubers and dark green leaves. In spring the flowers are produced above the leaves. Named varieties include 'Radar' (deep magenta with a white center), 'Violet Star' (purple with a white center), 'Atro-caerulea' (deep blue) and 'Charmer' (pink). Height and spread 6 in (15 cm). *A. nemerosa* (wood anemone) (zones 4-8) is low-growing, spreading by rhizome, with pale green leaves and single white flowers in spring. Height 6 in (15 cm), spread 12 in (30 cm).

Arisaema sikokianum (zones 5-9)

Tuberous perennial with dark green leaves, usually three- and five-lobed, producing a long, brown-purple spathe in spring. The white, stunted and club-like spadix is clearly visible in the base. Likes a sheltered site. Height 20 in (50 cm), spread 6 in (15 cm).

Arisarum proboscideum (zones 7-9)

Dense, spreading, rhizomatous perennial with shiny, dark green, arrow-shaped leaves. Flowers appear in spring and are often hidden by the foliage. Small hooded spathes have long thin tips, deep brown fading to white at the base. Height 6 in (15 cm), spread 12 in (30 cm).

Arum creticum (zones 8-10)

Lords and ladies are tuberous perennials with dark green, arrow-shaped leaves and deep yellow spathes in spring. They curve out at the tip, revealing a yellow and fragrant spadix. Height 18 in (45 cm), spread 8 in (20 cm).

Convallaria majalis (zones 2-7)

Lily of the valley is a rhizomatous perennial with pairs of shiny, mid-green, basal leaves and bell-shaped, waxy, white, heavily scented flowers on arching stems in late spring. Spreads rapidly to colonise large areas. Height and spread 10 in (25 cm). The variety *C. m.* 'Albostriata' has creamy white stripes on the leaves. *C. m.* 'Rosea' has lilac-pink flowers.

Crocosmia (zones 6-9)

Crocosmia 'Lucifer' is a strong-growing peren-nial from a corm, with sword-like, mid-green, ribbed leaves and long-stemmed spikes of upward-pointing clear red flowers in summer. Height 36 in (90 cm), spread 4 in (10 cm) but will quickly colonize a larger area. *C.* 'Solfatare'

Arum creticum

rapidly forms large clumps. It has bronze-green leaves and orange-yellow flowers in summer. Height 24 in (60 cm), spread 4 in (10 cm).

Cyclamen (zones 5-9)

Cyclamen cilicium is a tuberous perennial whose rounded, mid-green leaves have pale green patterns. The flowers are white or pink with a deep red stain at the mouth. A pure white form, *C. c.* 'Album', flowers in late summer and autumn, the leaves appear at the same time. Height 2 in (5 cm), spread 4 in (10 cm). *C. coum* has rounded, dark green leaves, often mottled with silver, appearing in winter and early spring with the deep pink, shuttlecock flowers. Height and spread 4 in (10 cm). *C. hederifolium* has ivy-shaped leaves mottled light and dark green with silver markings. The flowers appear just before the leaves in early to mid-winter and are icing-sugar pink with darker pink towards the mouth. Height and spread 6 in (15 cm).

Dahlia (zones 8-9)

Tuberous, half-hardy perennial, usually bushy, with good leaf cover. Can be grown

Right *Cyclamen coum*

Hyacinthoides hispanica

from the fleshy tubers, planted outdoors once the risk of frost is past, or from seed, to flower in the same year. There are 11 dahlia groups, based on flower shape, e.g. cactus, pompon and decorative. Leaves can be dull or glossy, pale, mid-or dark green on thick, pale green stems. Flowers are produced during summer and autumn in a range of colors from purest white to deepest red. Height ranges from the dwarf bedding at 6 in (15 cm) to 5 ft (1.5 m), with a spread of 12–24 in (30–60 cm).

Eranthis hyemalis (zones 4-9)
Winter aconite is a perennial with knobbly tubers and bright green circles of leaves below large, bright yellow flowers in late winter and early spring. Spreads quickly to form large clumps. Height and spread 2 in (5 cm).

Erythronium dens-canis (zones 3-9)
Dog's-tooth violet is a bulbous perennial with mid-green leaves heavily marked with purplish brown. White, pink or lilac flowers appear in spring. Height and spread 6 in (15 cm).

Fritillaria imperialis (zones 5-9)
Crown imperial is a bulbous perennial with

pale green leaves and umbels of bell-shaped flowers in late spring. The heads of 4–8 red, orange or yellow flowers are carried on long stems, have a strong foxy odor and are topped with a cluster of green bracts. Height 4 ft (1.2 m), spread 12 in (30 cm).

Galanthus nivalis (zones 3-9)
The common snowdrop is a bulbous perennial with narrow glaucous leaves and white flowers in winter. The inner tepals have an inverted V-shaped green tip and are slightly fragrant. Height and spread 4 in (10 cm).

Hyacinthoides (zones 4-9)
Hyacinthoides hispanica (Spanish bluebell) is a bulbous perennial with erect, strap-shaped, shiny, dark green leaves and bell-shaped blue flowers on long stalks in spring. *H. h.* 'Excelsior' has violet-blue flowers with a pale blue stripe. Height 20 in (50 cm), spread 4 in (10 cm). Quite rampant, quickly forming large drifts.
Hyacinthoides non-scripta (English bluebell) has long, glossy, dark green leaves and thin, bell-shaped bright blue (sometimes white), scented flowers in spring. The flower stem or raceme is one-sided and droops over at the tip. Height 12 in (30 cm), spread 4 in (10 cm), quickly spreading to cover large areas.

Oxalis
Oxalis adenophylla (zones 6-8) is a bulbous, clump-forming perennial with gray-green, heart-shaped leaves. In spring it produces funnel-shaped, deep pink, purple-veined flowers. Height 4 in (10 cm), spread 6 in (15 cm). *O. enneaphylla* (zones 6-9), a rhizomatous perennial with hairy, pleated, blue-gray leaves, flowers from spring to early summer in a range of shades from white to deep red. Height 4 in (10 cm), spread 6 in (15 cm).
Oxalis oregana (zones 7-9) is a rhizomatous, spreading perennial with hairy, mid-green leaves divided into heart-shaped leaflets. Flowers are produced from spring through to autumn in shades of white, pink or purple. Height 10 in (25 cm), spread indefinite.
Oxalis tetraphylla (good luck plant) (zones 8-9) is a bulbous perennial with leaves

resembling a four-leafed clover (hence the common name), with a purple blotch at the base of each leaflet. The flowers are pink-red with yellow centers and are produced all summer. Height and spread 8 in (20 cm).

Polygonatum
Polygonatum hirtum (zones 5-8) is a rhizomatous perennial with erect stems and mid-green leaves. The flowers hang down from the leaf axils from late spring until mid-summer and are creamy white with green tips. In autumn round black fruit are produced. Height 4 ft (1.2 m), spread 24 in (60 cm).
Polygonatum x hybridum (Solomon's seal) (zones 6-9) is a rhizomatous perennial with alternate lance-shaped mid-green leaves and green-tipped creamy white flowers in late spring, with round blue black fruit in autumn. Height 5 ft (1.5 m), spread 12 in (30 cm).

Trillium
Trillium cuneatum (zones 6-9) is a clump-forming, rhizomatous perennial. Mid-green leaves with pale green markings and stalkless maroon flowers with purple-tipped, dark green sepals smelling of musk appear in spring. Height 18 in (45 cm), spread 12 in (30 cm).
Trillium grandiflorum (wake robin) (zones 5-8) has long, dark green leaves. In spring and summer it produces pure white flowers that fade to pink, with bright green sepals just above the leaves. Height and spread 18 in (45 cm). *T. g.* 'Flore Pleno' is a lovely, double-flowered variety but is slower growing.
Trillium luteum (zones 5-8) has pointed mid-green leaves blotched with pale green. Deep yellow, sweetly scented flowers with pale green sepals are produced just above the leaves in spring. Height and spread 12 in (30 cm).

Zantedeschia aethiopica (zones 8-10)
Arum lily is a clump-forming perennial from rhizomes, with semi-erect, arrow-shaped, shiny green leaves that are evergreen in mild locations. The flowers are produced from early to mid-summer and are large and pure white, each with a pale yellow spadix. Height 36 in (90 cm), spread 24 in (60 cm).

FRUIT

Fruit is not normally associated with ground cover. The notable exception is the strawberry, though one or two others that are well worth growing are also listed here.

Vaccinium corymbosum

Fragaria (zones 5-9)

Many strawberries are evergreen and spread by runners, quickly covering large areas. The cultivated forms of strawberry are heavy croppers and successful ground coverers, forming a dense carpet. Summer strawberries, grown for their fruit and spreading by runners, are excellent for covering and holding soil and are ideal on a sunny bank.

The alpine strawberry, *Fragaria vesca*, has bright green leaves and white flowers in late spring followed by small, red, edible fruit. Height 12 in (30 cm), spread indefinite. *F. v.* 'Variegata' has dull green leaves splashed with white and cream. *F. v.* 'Semperflorens' is a treat to grow, producing tiny fruit with a strawberry smell as well as taste. It does not produce stolons, but forms a tight clump with pale green leaves and is grown from seed. 'Alexandria' is a good variety for fruit.

Fragaria 'Pink Panda' is a stoloniferous perennial with three palmate, mid-green leaves on long red-green stalks and bright pink flowers from mid-spring through to autumn. This plant seldom bears useful fruit. Height 6 in (15 cm), spread indefinite as the runners root readily in every direction. A good ground coverer with the ability to stabilise steep slopes. The variety *F.* 'Lipstick' has deep red blooms.

Rubus caesius (zones 7-9)

The dewberry is very popular in America, but despite an excellent flavor has never been widely grown in Britain. It is a distinct species, differing from the hybrid berries such as the tayberry, with which it is often included. It has three-lobed, pale green leaflets. The thin stems are well coated with thorns and scramble about, forming a dense carpet. Dewberry fruit are smaller than those of the blackberry and appear earlier, usually in mid-summer. The berries have a gray appearance caused by a surface bloom similar to a grape. If not supported the plant will spread for 10 ft (3 m) or more.

Vaccinium

Vaccinium angustifolium laevifolium (low bush blueberry) (zones 2-8) is a spreading, deciduous shrub with glossy, dark green leaves that turn red in autumn. White, bell-shaped flowers in late spring are followed by edible, sweet, blue-black berries. Height and spread 18 in (45 cm).

Vaccinium corymbosum (high bush blueberry) (zones 3-7) is a dense, deciduous shrub with light green leaves with good red or yellow autumn color. Racemes of white flowers in late spring are followed by edible, sweet, blue-black berries. Height and spread 5 ft (1.5 m).

Vaccinium macrocarpon (cranberry) (zones 2-7) is a prostrate, evergreen shrub with dark green leaves turning bronze in winter and bell-shaped pink flowers in summer followed by edible red berries. Height 6 in (15 cm), spread indefinite.

Vitis vinifera (zones 6-9)

Edible grape vine grown for its fruit. Happy to scramble over the ground, forming a tangled carpet of stems completely covered in large, pale green leaves from late spring through to late autumn. Without proper management most of the fruit will suffer from pests, diseases and vermin, but if what you want is ground cover, the leaves make it worth it. Spread can be over 33 ft (10 m).

Fragaria 'Pink Panda'

VEGETABLES

Lots of vegetables are good weed suppressers; growing main crop potatoes is an established practice for killing weeds. The dense leaf cover smothers weeds and is a good method of clearing ground prior to landscaping. Globe artichokes have bold architectural leaves ideal in mass planting or as dot plants in shrub and herbaceous borders.

Tetragonolobus purpureus

Brassica (Annual)
Although all the brassicas have masses of leaves that will deter weeds and form good ground cover, with the exception of the beautifully marked ornamental kale none is commonly used for ground cover. The main drawback of most of the bulky greens in this group is that just as they achieve maximum cover we pull them up and eat them. However, the ornamental kale is easily grown, providing great leaf colors including white, cream, pink, red and purple, from late summer right through autumn and winter when the temperature drops to below 50°F (10°C).

There are cabbage varieties to give you all-year ground cover, including 'Colorsa', a red-veined savoy, and red cabbage such as 'Red Jewel'. Well-grown cauliflowers (*Brassica oleracea*) are attractive with dark green leaves

surrounding a large, rounded curd of flowers that can be white, yellow-green or purple.

Cucurbita pepo (Annual)
Grown as annuals from seed, marrows come in many shapes and sizes of which the vegetable marrow, with its typical long cylindrical shape, is probably the most familiar. Courgettes are really just young marrows, although some modern varieties have been bred with more tender skin for picking small. The large, mid-green, divided leaves form good cover and the trailing varieties will extend 10 ft (3 m). Outdoor cucumbers have a smaller leaf, but provide good cover, producing long, narrow, green fruit. Squashes and pumpkins are available in a range of different shapes, colors and sizes of fruit, all with large leaves on strong, vine-like stems and spreading for 10 ft (3 m).

Cynara cardunculus Scolymus Group (zones 7-9)
Globe artichoke is a clump-forming perennial with enormous, deeply cut gray-green leaves and large, thistle-like, purple flower heads in late summer and autumn. Before the flower buds open to show color they can be cooked and eaten, and very nice they are too. Height 6 ft (2 m).

Pisum sativum (Annual)
Peas are annuals grown for their pods and seeds. Dwarf varieties can be used to cover the ground, reducing weeds during the summer months. It is essential that they are sown closely together to support each other and form a dense carpet. If the pods are not picked regularly the plant will stop growing and turn yellow.

Rheum x cultorum (zones 6-9)
Rhubarb, a fleshy-rooted perennial, has large, bright green leaves and edible, succulent stems (the leaves are poisonous). Tall spikes of flowers appear in early summer. A great vegetable for ground cover, adding interest to any mixed planting. Height and spread 4 ft (1.2 m).

Solanum tuberosum (Tender)
Potatoes are tuberous perennials with mid-green leaves on soft, pale green stems and with white, pink or blue flowers in summer. The tubers are edible and the skin color ranges from white through yellow to pink and purple. Frequently grown to break up hard, compacted soil and suppress weeds. Height 18 in (45 cm), spread 24 in (60 cm).

Tetragonolobus purpureus (zones 5-8)
Asparagus pea, an annual with pale green leaflets, is grown like a pea and eaten like a mangetout but is really a vetch. The flowers are scarlet-brown followed by oddly shaped, four-angled pods with frilled wings that are edible when eaten young. They need to be picked over frequently. Height 12 in (30 cm), spread 24 in (60 cm).

Pumpkin 'Baby Bear'

ALPINES

Rock garden plants and alpines should not really be included in this book at all. Any self-respecting, decent-sized perennial weed should be able to force its way through most such plants. Often, however, the plants listed here are used to bulk up the rockery, tumbling over rock and scree and helping to reduce the population of annual weeds. Their seeds, carried by wind, are trapped in the foliage and die long before their roots can reach the soil. It is best to treat these plants as edging cover, as they will suffer the same fate as weeds under taller dense cover. Alpines and rockery plants do make a bold show in very poor soil that is lacking in nutrients and moisture and can tolerate extreme temperatures.

As with the section on herbs, the plants described here are only those most useful as alpines. Other plants are covered under headings more appropriate to their use.

Alchemilla alpina (zones 3-7)
Alpine lady's mantle is a carpeting perennial with green, silver-edged, divided leaves. The flowers are yellowish green, in clusters on short stalks in summer. Height 6 in (15 cm) spread 24 in (60 cm).

Alyssum montanum (zones 4-9)
Mountain alison, a prostrate evergreen perennial, has gray, oval-shaped rosettes of leaves and golden yellow, scented flowers in early summer. It needs a well-drained sunny site and grows to 6 in (15 cm), spreading to 20 in (50 cm). *A. wulfenianum* is very similar.

Andromeda polifolia 'Alba' (zones 2-6)
Bog rosemary is a tough evergreen shrub with thin, leathery, dark green leaves. Flowers are white and appear in spring and summer. Bog rosemary requires a moist acid soil. Height and spread 12 in (30 cm).

Antennaria dioica rosea (zones 5-9)
Almost evergreen prostrate perennial with dull green leaves white on the underside and deep pink flowers in late spring and early summer. Height 4 in (10 cm), spread 18 in (45 cm).

Anthyllis montana (zones 6-8)
Carpet-forming perennial with small, finely divided, silvery green leaves. Tight heads of flowers, rather like clover flowers, appear in early summer in shades of pink or purple. Height 12 in (30 cm), spread 36 in (90 cm).

Arabis caucasica 'Variegata' (zones 4-8)
Carpeting evergreen perennial with rosettes of green leaves edged creamy yellow and scented spring flowers of clear white. It will tolerate poor, dry, infertile soils. Height 6 in (15 cm), spread 24 in (60 cm).

Arctostaphylos uva-ursi (zones 2-6)
Common bearberry is a carpet-forming evergreen shrub with leathery, dark green leaves and tiny pinkish white flowers in summer followed by deep red berries. Height 4 in (10 cm), spread 24 in (60 cm).

Asarina procumbens (zones 6-9)
Creeping snapdragon is an evergreen perennial that trails over the ground. It has sticky, gray-green, hairy leaves and creamy yellow flowers, with a darker yellow throat in summer. Grows to 2 in (5 cm) and spreads to 36 in (90 cm).

Aster alpinus (zones 5-7)
The perennial alpine aster spreads its thin, almost evergreen, mid-green leaves across 18 in (45 cm) and grows to 12 in (30 cm). The large, daisy-like flowers, light purple with a central yellow disc, appear in early to midsummer.

Aubretia x cultorum 'Argenteovariegata' (zones 5-7)
Evergreen, carpet-forming perennial with oval, toothed green leaves with white margins and deep pink flowers in spring. Height 2 in (5 cm). The variety *A.* x *c.* 'J. S. Baker' is of similar growth but has purple flowers with a white eye.

Aurinia saxatilis 'Citrina' (zones 4-8)
A perennial forming an evergreen mound. Has gray-green leaves with pale yellow flowers in late spring and early summer. Height 8 in (20 cm), spread 18 in (45 cm).

Campanula (zones 4-7)
Campanula 'Birch Hybrid' is a fast, low-growing, evergreen perennial with bright green leaves and mauve-blue bell flowers covering the plant in summer. Grows to 6 in (15 cm), spreading to 18 in (45 cm). *C. portenschlagiana* has mid-green leaves and deep blue flowers all summer. Height 6 in (15 cm), spread 18 in (45 cm).

Arabis caucasica 'Variegata'

Celmisia walkeri (zones 9-10)
An evergreen perennial from New Zealand with dark green, leathery leaves. The flowers are white with a yellow center in early summer. Height and spread 12 in (30 cm).

Clematis marmoraria (zones 6-9)
Prostrate, evergreen shrub with shiny, dark green, divided leaves. The flowers are

greenish white in early spring, becoming creamy white as they age, and are followed by fluffy white seed heads. Grows to 6 in (15 cm), spread 12 in (30 cm).

Cornus canadensis (zones 2-7)

Creeping dogwood, an evergreen perennial, has bright green leaves and small green flowers with white bracts in late spring, followed by bright red berries. Requires an acid, moist soil in shade. Reaching 6 in (15 cm) in height, it spreads all over the place and needs to be kept in check.

Daphne

Daphne alpina (zones 6-8) is a deciduous shrub with dull green leaves and fragrant white flowers in late spring, followed by deep orange berries. Height and spread 24 in (60 cm). *D. arbuscula* (zones 5-7) is a prostrate evergreen with shiny, leathery, dark green leaves and marvellously perfumed deep pink flowers in spring and early summer. Height 6 in (15 cm), spread 20 in (50 cm). *D. blagayana* (zones 7-9) is also evergreen, with leathery, dark green leaves and creamy white, sweetly scented flowers in spring, followed by white or pale pink berries. Height 18 in (45 cm), spread 36 in (90 cm). *D. cneorum* (garland

Eriogonum umbellatum

Daphne blagayana

flower) (zones 5-7), a low-growing, spreading evergreen, has dark green leaves and terminal clusters of fragrant pink flowers in spring. Height 8 in (20 cm), spread 6 ft (180 cm).

Dianthus

Dianthus erinaceus (hedgehog pink) (zones 4-8) forms a dense, perennial, evergreen cushion that looks a bit like a hedgehog, with thin, light green leaves and star-like pink flowers in summer. Height 2 in (5 cm), spread 24 in (60 cm). *D. gratiano-politanus* (Cheddar pink) (zones 3-8) is a carpeting, evergreen perennial with gray-green leaves and deep pink, perfumed flowers in summer. Height 6 in (15 cm), spread 18 in (45 cm).

Dionysia involucrata (zones 5-7)

Forms a tight, evergreen cushion of dark green leaves and large, rosy pink, red-centered flowers in early summer. Height 4 in (10 cm), spread 10 in (25 cm).

Erigeron karvinskianus (zones 5-7)

A vigorous, evergreen perennial that quickly forms clumps with dull green leaves and daisy-like flowers in summer. Blooms open white with a yellow center turning through pink to purple as they age. Grows to 8 in (20 cm) high with a spread of 36 in (90 cm).

Erinacea anthyllis (zones 7-8)

This low-growing, evergreen shrub requiring well-drained soil, has small, dark green leaves

on green stems. The flowers, which appear in early summer, are a pale purple-blue. Height 12 in (30 cm), spread 36 in (90 cm)

Eriogonum umbellatum (zones 4-8)

Sulphur flower is a low-growing, evergreen perennial. Its leaves are light green with white on the reverse. Clusters of tiny pale yellow flowers are produced in summer. Height 12 in (30 cm), spread 36 in (90 cm).

Euphorbia myrsinites (zones 6-8)

Carpeting evergreen perennial. The fleshy, blue-green leaves form spirals on the prostrate stems. Greenish yellow flowers are produced at the ends of the stems in spring. Height 4 in (10 cm), spread 24 in (60 cm).

Euryops acraeus (zones 7-10)

Evergreen shrub with waxy silver leaves and bright yellow, daisy-type flowers in summer. It needs a well-drained site protected from winter rain. Height and spread 18 in (45 cm).

Gaultheria procumbens (zones 3-7)

Wintergreen has leathery, dark green leaves that are aromatic when broken. This creeping evergreen shrub has pale pink, sometimes white, summer flowers, followed by bright red berries. Height 6 in (15 cm), spread 36 in (90 cm).

Genista pilosa 'Procumbens' (zones 6-9)

Low-growing deciduous shrub with thin, dark green leaves and orange-yellow flowers in summer. Height 10 in (25 cm), spread 24 in (60 cm).

Gentiana verna (zones 4-7)

Spring gentian is a carpet-forming, evergreen perennial with dark green leaves and tubular sky-blue flowers with white throats in spring and summer. Height 2 in (5 cm), spread 4 in (10 cm).

Helianthemum (zones 6-8)

Helianthemum apenninum (rock rose), a low-growing evergreen shrub with gray-green

■ **Right** *Daphne arbuscula*

leaves, produces white flowers with deep yellow centers in late spring and early summer. Height 18 in (45 cm), spread 24 in (60 cm).

Helianthemum 'Rhodanthe Carneum' used to be called *H.* 'Wisley Pink' and is a low-spreading evergreen shrub with silver-gray leaves. The flowers are pale pink with an apricot center and are produced from late spring into early summer. Height 12 in (30 cm), spread 18 in (45 cm). *H.* 'Wisley Primrose' is one of the best of the rock roses, quickly spreading over the ground. It is an evergreen shrub with dull green leaves and pale yellow flowers with deep yellow centers and is in bloom from late spring until mid-summer. Height 12 in (30 cm), spread 24 in (60 cm).

Omphalodes cappadocica

Horminum pyrenaicum (zones 6-8)
Dragon's mouth is an evergreen perennial with shiny, leathery, dark green leaves that form basal rosettes. The dark blue flowers appear all summer. Height 10 in (25 cm), spread 20 in (50 cm).

Hypericum cerastioides (zones 6-7)
An evergreen sub-shrub that has soft, light green leaves and large, deep yellow, star-shaped flowers in early summer. Height 6 in (15 cm), spread 18 in (45 cm).

Iberis sempervirens (zones 5-9)
A low, spreading, evergreen sub-shrub with dark green leaves. The flowers that appear in late spring and early summer are pure white, occasionally tinged with pink. Height 12 in (30 cm), spread 20 in (50 cm).

Linnaea borealis (zones 2-6)
Evergreen sub-shrub that forms a low carpet of paired, shiny, dark green leaves. The flowers are bell-shaped, pale pink and appear in summer. Height 4 in (10 cm), spread 3 ft (1 m).

Lithodora diffusa 'Heavenly Blue'
(zones 6-8)
Evergreen shrub that quickly forms a low hummock. Its leaves are glossy and dark green. Deep blue flowers in terminal clusters appear in late spring and early summer. Requires an acid soil. Height 6 in (15 cm), spread 24 in (60 cm).

Lysimachia nummularia 'Aurea' (zones 4-8)
Golden creeping Jenny is a prostrate and rampant, stem-rooting, evergreen perennial with an indefinite spread. The leaves are paired, rounded and bright yellow and it has buttercup yellow flowers in summer. Height 2 in (5 cm).

Omphalodes cappadocica (zones 6-8)
Evergreen perennial forming a compact clump with small, pointed, ferny green leaves. In spring it has bright sky blue flowers with a white center like forget-me-nots. Height 10 in (25 cm), spread 24 in (60 cm).

Penstemon rupicola (zones 4-9)
Rock penstemon is a prostrate evergreen sub-shrub with thick, leathery, dark green leaves. The flowers that appear in late spring and early summer are dark purple-pink and funnel shaped. Height 4 in (10 cm), spread 18 in (45 cm).

Phlox stolonifera (zones 4-8)
Creeping phlox, a spreading herbaceous perennial, has dark green leaves and pale or deep purple flowers in early summer. Height 6 in (15 cm), spread 12 in (30 cm).

Phyllodoce
Phyllodoce caerulea (mountain heath) (zones 2-5) is a dwarf evergreen shrub with shiny, dark green leaves. Bell-shaped flowers are pink-purple from spring to early summer. Height 10 in (25 cm), spread 12 in (30 cm). *P. empetriformis* (zones 3-6) is a carpet-forming evergreen with bright green leaves and pink-purple, bell-shaped flowers carried on long stems in early summer. Height 12 in (30 cm), spread 18 in (45 cm).

Pratia pedunculata (zones 5-7)
In Australia this is a bit of a weed and if you are not careful it will be a weed in your garden also. It is a flat-growing, vigorous, evergreen perennial with shiny green leaves and pale blue flowers with white centers in summer. Height 1 in (25 mm).

Rhodanthemum hormariense (zones 8-10)
Spreading evergreen sub-shrub with silvery green leaves and white daisy flowers. Height and spread 12 in (30 cm).

Sedum
Sedum rupestre (zones 6-9) forms a matted evergreen perennial with fleshy, gray-green, pointed leaves and orange-yellow flowers in summer on upright stems held above the foliage. Height 4 in (10 cm), spread 24 in (60 cm). The fleshy leaves of *S. spathulifolium* 'Cape Blanco' (zones 5-9) form silvery green rosettes with a white bloom. The flowers are yellow and clustered above the leaves. Height 4 in (10 cm), spread 32 in (80 cm).

Verbascum dumulosum (zones 6-9)
Evergreen sub-shrub with downy stems and gray, heavily felted leaves. The flowers are bright yellow with brick-red centers on short stems in summer. Height 10 in (25 cm), spread 36 in (90 cm).

Veronica peduncularis (zones 6-8)
Carpeting perennial with shiny, deep green leaves, tinted purple. The long sprays of flowers can be white, pink or dark blue in spring and summer. Height 6 in (15 cm), spread 24 in (60 cm).

HERBACEOUS PERENNIALS

A herbaceous plant is defined as one that has soft (rather than hard, woody) growth and can be annual, biennial or perennial. A perennial is a plant that lives more than three seasons or two years, and once mature flowers annually.

Herbaceous perennials therefore cover an enormous range of plants of all shapes and sizes that will screen the ground and reduce weeds. In order to simplify the search for a plant to suit your requirements this section is sub-divided into two categories, low-growing and medium. Low includes plants to 24 in (60 cm) high; medium more than 24 in (60 cm). For the purpose of this book I am omitting perennial plants that don't spread, or spread very slowly. Those appearing late in the season and hibernating early are also excluded. But don't worry – there are more than enough left for everyone to share.

Herbaceous plants have as diverse a selection of leaves as any other group and more than most. It is difficult to find similarities between Gunnera manicata *with its enormous, deciduous, rough-surfaced, light green leaves 6 ft 6 in (2 m) across and* Stachys olympica, *whose common name 'lambs ears' aptly describes the 4 in (10 cm) long, gray-green, furry leaves.*

Many herbaceous plants are evergreen, including Bergenia, Helleborus, Heuchera *and* Myosotidium *(my favorite, favorite plant in this group) and as such are invaluable for weed control year round, as they present a brave leafy face even in the dead of winter.*

Even down the scale from Gunnera *there are lots of other bold-leaved herbaceous plants. The rhubarb family gives us* Rheum officinale *and* R. palmatum *with super leaves and enormous spikes of cream flowers.* Lysichiton americanum *has large leaves to set off its arum flowers and* Rodgersia podophylla *has leaves to make any chestnut jealous. Interestingly, all these large-leaved herbaceous plants prefer a deep, moist-to-wet soil. In full sun* Rodgersia *leaves will color to a deep red-bronze.*

Herbaceous perennials are perhaps the easiest of all plants to propagate. Many of the carpeters spread rapidly, rooting as they go and allowing you to take an 'Irishman's cutting' (see page 31). These cuttings can be planted into any gaps in your ground-covering. Watered in with a little compost and bone meal they will soon fill the allotted space.

LOW-GROWING

Aegopodium podagraria 'Variegatum' (zones 4-9)
Variegated bishop's weed. This 'weed' is one of the best plants for covering the ground. It is a perennial with lobed, creamy white variegated leaves and small white flowers in summer. Height 8 in (20 cm), spread indefinite.

Ajuga reptans 'Multicolor' (zones 3-9)
Evergreen ground-covering perennial that rapidly spreads to form a dense carpet of rosettes of bronze-green leaves mottled with pink and cream. The deep blue flowers are carried on short stems in late spring and early summer. Height 6 in (15 cm) spread 36 in (90 cm). *A. r.* 'Variegata' has gray-green leaves splashed with cream. *A. r.* 'Burgundy Glow' has silver-green leaves mottled with deep red.

Alchemilla
Alchemilla conjuncta (zones 3-7) is a clump-forming perennial with small star-shaped leaves, mid-green with pale edges and green-yellow flowers in summer. Height and spread 12 in (30 cm). *A. mollis* (lady's mantle) (zones 4-7) is a great ground-coverer with pale green, wavy-edged leaves that hold beads of water like drops of mercury. The flowers are green-yellow, small and displayed in dainty sprays in summer. Height and spread 24 in (60 cm).

Anemone
Anemone ranunculoides (zones 4-8) is a fast-spreading perennial with pale green leaves on short stems and deep yellow, buttercup-like flowers in spring. Height and spread 10 in (25 cm). *A. sylvestris* (snowdrop windflower) (zones 4-9) is an invasive creeping perennial with mid-green, divided leaves and fragrant white flowers with yellow centers in late spring and early summer. Height and spread 12 in (30 cm).

Anthemis punctata cupaniana (zones 6-9)
Evergreen, carpeting perennial with silvery foliage that becomes green in winter. The daisy-like white flowers have yellow centers and are on show all summer. Height and spread 12 in (30 cm).

Artemisia schmidtiana (zones 5-8)
Low-growing, evergreen perennial with silky, hairy leaves and panicles of small yellow flowers in summer. Height 12 in (30 cm), spread 18 in (45 cm).

Aster amellus 'King George'

Asarum europaeum (zones 4-8)
Asarabacca is a creeping evergreen perennial with glossy, dark green leaves and bell-shaped, greenish-yellow flowers that turn pale brown in late spring. Height 4 in (10 cm), spread 12 in (30 cm).

Aster
Aster amellus 'King George', (zones 5-8) a bushy perennial with dark green leaves, produces violet-blue, daisy-like flowers with yellow centers in late summer and autumn. Height and spread 24 in (60 cm).
Aster novi-belgii 'Royal Ruby' (zones 4-8) is a dwarf bushy perennial with mid-green foliage, prone to mildew attacks, but still worth growing. The flowers are deep red and daisy-like in autumn. Height and spread 18 in (45 cm).

Astilbe 'Fanal' (zones 4-9)
Bushy perennial with good dark green leaf cover and feathery plumes of tiny, deep red flowers in summer. Height 24 in (60 cm), spread 36 in (90 cm).

Astrantia major (zones 4-7)
Clump-forming perennial with a mass of mid-green leaves and, in summer, green-white flowers with a hint of pink. Height 24 in (60 cm), spread 18 in (45 cm).

Bergenia
Bergenia ciliata (zones 5-8) is an evergreen with large, hairy, rounded leaves, Clusters of flowers – white in spring, turning pink as they age – are carried on thick stems. Height 12 in (30 cm), spread 24 in (60 cm).
Bergenia cordifolia 'Purpurea' (elephant's ears) (zones 3-8) is an evergreen, clump-forming perennial with deep green, purple-tinged leaves. The rosy pink clusters of flowers bloom from late winter through to spring. Height and spread 20 in (50 cm).

Left Ground cover can be an effective foil for more striking plants. Here, delphiniums grow up through a carpet of *Alchemilla mollis* and two varieties of *Centaurea*.

Calceolaria 'John Innes'

Bergenia 'Silberlicht' (silver light) (zones 3-8), an evergreen, clump-forming perennial, has mid-green leaves with serrated margins and clusters of white flowers on stiff stems in spring. Height 12 in (30 cm), spread 24 in (60 cm).

Brunnera macrophylla 'Variegata' (zones 3-7)
Ground-covering perennial with creamy white heart-shaped leaves and small, bright blue flowers in spring. Height 18 in (45 cm), spread 24 in (60 cm).

Buphthalmum salicifolium (zones 3-7)
Yellow ox-eye is a spreading perennial with small mid-green leaves and single, deep yellow flowers all summer long. Height 24 in (60 cm), spread 36 in (90 cm).

Calceolaria 'John Innes' (zones 5-8)
Quick-growing, evergreen perennial with basal mid-green leaves and large deep yellow flowers in the shape of a pouch, speckled brown in late spring and early summer. Height 8 in (20 cm), spread 12 in (30 cm).

Catananche caerulea (zones 3-7)
Clump-forming perennial with gray-green grassy leaves and daisy-like mid-blue flowers in summer. Height 18 in (45 cm), spread 12 in (30 cm).

Centaurea montana (zones 3-8)
Spreading perennial with mid-green leaves and flowers that can be white, pink, blue or purple with thistle-like centers and an outer ring of radiating petals. Height and spread 24 in (60 cm).

Cerastium tomentosum (zones 3-7)
Snow in summer is a rampant, evergreen, carpet-forming perennial with woolly white leaves and masses of star-shaped, white flowers in late spring and summer. Height 2 in (5 cm), spread indefinite.

Convallaria majalis (lily of the valley) (zones 2-7)
See under **Bulbs**, page 108.

Coreopsis verticillata (zones 4-9)
Bushy perennial with dark green leaves and a mass of golden-yellow flowers all summer. Height 18 in (45 cm), spread 12 in (30 cm).

Crambe maritima (zones 6-9)
Seakale is a strong-growing perennial with silvery green leaves and masses of small white flowers that are fragrant in summer. Height and spread 24 in (60 cm).

Dianthus deltoides (zones 3-8)
Maiden pink is a carpet-forming perennial with narrow, dark green leaves and single flowers with bearded petals in white, pink

and deep red. Height 8 in (20 cm), spread 12 in (30 cm). The variety *D. d.* 'Flashing Light' has bright cerise flowers.

Diascia rigescens (zones 7-9)
Trailing semi-evergreen perennial with dull green leaves and racemes of deep pink flowers in summer. Height 12 in (30 cm), spread 24 in (60 cm).

Epimedium
Epimedium pubigerum (zones 5-9) is evergreen and carpet-forming, with dense, heart-shaped foliage and clusters of white flowers in spring. Height and spread 18 in (45 cm). *E.* x *rubrum* (zones 4-8) also forms a carpet and has heart-shaped, mid-green leaves that are blotched with brown-red in early spring. The flowers are deep red with bright yellow spurs in spring. Height and spread 10 in (25 cm).

Erigeron 'Charity' (zones 5-8)
Clump-forming perennial with mid-green leaves and daisy-like pale pink flowers all summer. Height and spread 24 in (60 cm).

Eriophyllum lanatum (zones 5-8)
Cushion type of perennial with small, silvery leaves and daisy-like yellow flowers all summer. Height and spread 12 in (30 cm)

Erodium manescavii (zones 6-8)
Clump-forming perennial with ferny, dark green leaves and deep pink flowers all summer. Height 18 in (45 cm), spread 24 in (60 cm).

Euphorbia
Euphorbia amygdaloides robbiae (zones 6-9) is a spreading evergreen with dark green leaves and yellow-green flowers in spring. Height 18 in (45 cm), spread 24 in (60 cm). *E. cyparissias*, another spreader, has a mass of gray-green leaves and lime-green flower bracts in spring. Height 12 in (30 cm), spread indefinite. *E. polychroma* (zones 4-9) is bushy with mid-green leaves and shiny yellow flowers in spring. Height and spread 24 in (60 cm).

Filipendula ulmaria 'Aurea' (zones 3-9)
Perennial with a good mass of golden yellow leaves in spring, turning light green in summer. The flowers are creamy white, forming sprays in summer. Height and spread 12 in (30 cm).

Gentiana x macaulayi 'Wells's Variety' (zones 5-7)
Rosette-forming, semi-evergreen perennial with dark green basal leaves. Trumpet-shaped pale blue flowers are pale striped on the outside of the trumpet in late summer and autumn. Height 2 in (5 cm), spread 12 in (30 cm).

Geranium
Geranium endressii (zones 5-8) is a semi-evergreen carpeting perennial with small, glossy dark green leaves and cup-shaped, deep rose-pink flowers all summer. Height 18 in (45 cm), spread 24 in (60 cm). The variety *G. e.* 'Wargrave Pink' has salmon pink flowers.
   The vigorous *Geranium* 'Johnson's Blue' (zones 4-8) has mid-green divided leaves and cup-shaped, deep blue flowers in summer. Height 12 in (30 cm), spread 24 in (60 cm).
   Geranium macrorrhizum 'Ingwersen's Variety' (zones 4-8) forms an excellent ground-covering carpet with aromatic mid-green leaves that turn brown-red in autumn. The flowers are pale pink in late spring and summer. Height 12 in (30 cm), spread 24 in (60 cm).
   Geranium nodosum (zones 4-8) is a clump-forming perennial with shiny green leaves and lilac-pink flowers in late spring and summer. Height and spread 18 in (45 cm).
   Geranium pratense 'Kashmir White' (zones 4-8) is another carpeter with dark green divided leaves. The white, cup-shaped flowers with lilac veins appear all summer. Height and spread 24 in (60 cm).
   Geranium sanguineum striatum (zones 4-8) forms compact clumps with bright green leaves and pale, dark-veined pink flowers in summer. Height 4 in (10 cm), spread 12 in (30 cm).

Geum x borisii (zones 5-8)
Clump-forming perennial with dull green

Eriophyllum lanatum

leaves and bright orange flowers with yellow stamens carried on long stems during summer. Height and spread 18 in (45 cm).

Glechoma hederacea 'Variegata' (zones 5-9)
Variegated ground ivy is an evergreen carpeting perennial with small, heart-shaped leaves and white markings. Flowers are insignificant. Height 6 in (15 cm), spread indefinite.

Helleborus
The three species listed here are all clump-forming evergreens.
   Helleborus orientalis (zones 4-9) has pale green, divided foliage and cup-shaped, purple, pink or white flowers in winter or early spring. Height and spread 18 in (45 cm).
   Helleborus argutifolius (Corsican hellebore) (zones 6-9) has spiny, dark green leaves and large clusters of pale green flowers in winter and early spring. Height 24 in (60 cm), spread 18 in (45 cm).
   Helleborus niger (the Christmas rose) (zones 4-8) has overwintering thick, leathery, dark green leaves and white-green flowers in winter and early spring. The flowers are often flushed with pink. Height 12 in (30 cm), spread 18 in (45 cm).

Hosta 'Ground Master'

Hemerocallis 'Mini Pearl' (zones 3-9)
Daylily is a compact, free-flowering evergreen perennial with strap-like glossy leaves and large white flowers flushed pink in early summer. Height and spread 18 in (45 cm). There are many varieties, most of which produce flowers that last for only one day. Those in the 'Siloam' range are compact and evergreen.

Heuchera
Another useful group of evergreens.
Heuchera 'Palace Purple' (zones 4-8) has deep purple, heart-shaped leaves and delicate white sprays of flowers in summer. Height and spread 18 in (45 cm).
The leaves of *Heuchera* 'Red Spangles' (zones 3-8), also heart-shaped, are purple-green and the plant produces bell-shaped scarlet flowers in summer. Height and spread 12 in (30 cm).

Heuchera x *Heucherella* 'Bridget Bloom' is a clump-former with a mass of bright green leaves and sprays of tiny rosy red flowers from early summer through until autumn. Height and spread 18 in (45 cm). *H.* x *Heucherella tiarelloides* (zones 5-8) is ideal as ground cover, with masses of shiny green leaves and sprays of bell-shaped, small pink flowers in early summer. Height and spread 18 in (45 cm).

Hosta (zones 3-9)
Hostas or plantain lilies are marvellous plants with bold leaves, forming large clumps with a dense, matted root system that in itself deters weeds. They prefer damp, shady conditions and a rich, well-drained soil, but are very prone to slug and snail damage. Hostas are all clump-forming deciduous perennials and the following is a selection of low-growing varieties.

Hosta 'August Moon' has heart-shaped, puckered, pale green leaves turning yellow in early summer. The flowers are a dirty white. Height 20 in (50 cm), spread 30 in (75 cm).
Hosta 'Big Daddy' has heart-shaped, glaucous gray-blue leaves and gray-white flowers. Height 24 in (60 cm), spread 36 in (90 cm). *H. crispula* has lance-shaped, dark green leaves with twisted tips and with white margins. Flowers are blue-white in summer. Height 20 in (50 cm), spread 36 in (90 cm).
Hosta fortunei has dark green leaves with mauve flowers on long stems in summer. Height 20 in (50 cm), spread 36 in (90 cm). *H. f. aureomarginata* has leathery deep green leaves margined with yellow. The flowers are mauve in mid-summer. Height 20 in (50 cm), spread 36 in (90 cm).
Hosta 'Golden Tiara' has mid-green leaves irregularly edged with yellow and bell-shaped, deep purple flowers. Height 12 in (30 cm), spread 24 in (60 cm). The variety 'Ground Master' is prostrate, spreading by stolons. The dull green leaves have cream margins and the flowers are funnel-shaped, deep purple in summer. Height 12 in (30 cm), spread 24 in (60 cm). 'Halycon' has bright gray-blue leaves and bell-shaped, lavender blue flowers in summer. Height 16 in (40 cm), spread 30 in (75 cm).
Hosta 'True Blue' has heart-shaped, glaucous gray-blue leaves and dirty-white flowers in summer. Height 24 in (60 cm), spread 36 in (90 cm). 'Wide Brim' has heart-shaped, dark green leaves marked on the leaf edge with cream. The flowers are pale lavender blue in summer. Height 18 in (45 cm), spread 36 in (90 cm).
Hosta 'Zounds' shows considerable resistance to slug and snail damage. The leaves are heart-shaped, thick and deep yellow with a metallic sheen that perhaps gives the poor slugs indigestion. The flowers are pale lavender blue. Height 20 in (50 cm), spread 36 in (90 cm).

Houttuynia cordata 'Chamaeleon' (zones 3-8)
Vigorous deciduous perennial, excellent for ground cover, that can be grown as a marginal water plant. Leathery, aromatic

mid-green leaves are splashed with pink, red and yellow. The flowers are white in summer. Height 4 in (10 cm), spread indefinite.

Kniphofia

The evergreen *Kniphofia hirsuta* (torch lily, red hot poker) (zones 7-9) has hairy, dark green leaves that are red at the base and pale red flowers that turn yellow in typical 'poker' racemes in spring. Height 18 in (45 cm), spread 24 in (60 cm). *K.* 'Little Maid' (zones 6-9) is a deciduous perennial with thin, grass-like leaves and pale, lime green flowers that turn pale yellow and then creamy white in late summer and early autumn. Height 24 in (60 cm), spread 18 in (45 cm).

Lamium (zones 4-8)

Lamium galeobdolon (yellow archangel). How this plant could possibly be described as an archangel I just don't know. It is a very invasive perennial spreading by stolons with mid-green toothed leaves often marked with silver. The spikes of yellow flowers are produced in summer. Height 24 in (60 cm), spread indefinite. *L. g.* 'Silver Angel', with its silver leaves, is slightly less invasive and, at 18 in (45 cm), lower growing.

Lamium maculatum (dead nettle) is a low-

Houttuynia cordata 'Chamaeleon'

growing perennial, spreading by stolons to form a solid carpet of mid-green leaves with a white or pale pink blotch and red, pink or white flowers in summer. Height 8 in (20 cm), spread 36 in (90 cm). There are many varieties, including 'White Nancy', with pure white flowers and silver leaves margined green; 'Beacon Silver', with similar leaves but pale pink flowers; and 'Aureum', which has pink flowers above yellow leaves with white centers.

Lathyrus vernus (zones 5-9)

Clump-forming with ferny foliage and small purple and blue flowers in spring. Height and spread 10 in (25 cm).

Limonium latifolium 'Blue Cloud' (zones 4-9)

Clump-forming with dark green, leathery leaves and clouds of purple-blue flowers in late summer. Height and spread 18 in (45 cm).

Linum narborense (zones 6-9)

Clump-forming with gray-green leaves and blue flowers in late spring and early summer. Height and spread 12 in (30 cm).

Lychnis

Lychnis coronaria (zones 4-8), a perennial often grown as a biennial, has soft gray leaves and flat cerise-crimson flowers on long gray stems in mid-summer. Height 24 in (60 cm), spread 18 in (45 cm). *L. flos-jovis* (zones 6-9) is a perennial with gray-green foliage and deep pink flowers in the height of summer. Height and spread 20 in (50 cm). *L. viscaria* 'Splendens Plena' (zones 4-8) is a clump-forming perennial with large mid-green leaves. The base leaves are covered in sticky hairs. Double magenta flowers appear in early summer. Height 18 in (45 cm), spread 12 in (30 cm).

Lysimachia nummularia 'Aurea' (zones 4-8)

See under Alpines, page 116.

Meconopsis quintuplinervia (zones 7-8)

Harebell poppy forms a dense carpet of large, pale green leaves and sky blue flowers, deep blue at the base in spring and early summer. Height and spread 12 in (30 cm).

Myosotidium hortensia

Mimulus

Mimulus guttatus (zones 6-9) spreads vigorously by stolons, with mid-green leaves and funnel-shaped flowers with red throats in summer. Height 12 in (30 cm), spread 36 in (90 cm). *M. luteus* (monkey musk) (zones 7-9) is a spreading perennial with mid-green leaves. Yellow flowers spotted with deep red on the petal lobes are produced in summer. Height 12 in (30 cm), spread 24 in (60 cm).

Mitella stauropetala (zones 4-8)

Bishop's cap is vigorous with purple-tinged, light green leaves and small white or purple flowers on long stems during summer. Height 24 in (60 cm), spread 12 in (30 cm).

Myosotidium hortensia (zones 8-9)

Chatham Island forget-me-not is my favorite herbaceous plant, an evergreen with very large, shiny, ribbed, mid-green leaves and enormous clusters of wedgwood blue flowers in late spring and early summer. Not suitable for cold, exposed sites. Height 18 in (45 cm), spread 24 in (60 cm).

Nepeta (zones 4-8)

Nepeta x *faassenii* (catmint) forms clumps of aromatic, wrinkled, gray-green leaves that cats just love to roll in. Lavender blue flowers with deep blue spots appear from

Pachyphragma macrophyllum

early summer until mid-autumn. Height and spread 18 in (45 cm). *N. phyllochlamys* (zones 8-9) is a spreading species with aromatic, pale gray-green leaves. Purple-pink flowers with white bracts appear in summer. Height 4 in (10 cm), spread 12 in (30 cm).

Osteospermum jucundum (zones 9-10)
Also known as *Dimorphotheca barberiae*, this is a clump-former with grayish-green leaves and large daisy-like flowers on long stems from late spring until autumn. The radiating florets are mauve-pink to purple, with purple-pink on the reverse. The purple disc florets turn gold with age. Height 18 in (45 cm), spread 36 in (90 cm).

Ourisia microphylla (zones 5-7)
Carpet-forming evergreen with small, pale green leaves and small, pale pink flowers in late spring and early summer. Height 2 in (5 cm), spread 8 in (20 cm).

Pachyphragma macrophyllum (zones 5-9)
Creeping, carpet-former with shiny, bright green leaves and racemes of small white flowers in spring. Height 12 in (30 cm), spread indefinite.

Pachysandra terminalis (zones 4-8)
Spreading evergreen with shiny, dark green leaves and tiny white flowers in spring. Height 10 in (25 cm), spread indefinite. The variety *P. t.* 'Green Carpet' is more compact, growing to 6 in (15 cm) high. *P. t.* 'Variegata' has white-margined leaves and is slow-growing, reaching a height of 12 in (30 cm) and a spread of 24 in (60 cm).

Paronychia (zones 8-10)
Paronychia capitata is a vigorous carpeting plant with silvery green leaves and small green flowers surrounded by silvery bracts in summer. Height 2 in (5 cm), spread 12 in (30 cm). *P. kapela* has silvery blue leaves and tiny greenish-white flowers with white papery bracts. Height 2 in (5 cm), spread 10 in (25 cm).

Persicaria
Persicaria affinis (zones 3-8) is a carpet-forming evergreen, with dark green leaves that turn red-bronze in autumn. Bright red flowers that fade to pale pink bloom from early summer to autumn. In winter the flower spikes turn a rich brown, giving winter color. Height 12 in (30 cm), spread 24 in (60 cm). *P. capitata* (zones 7-8), also evergreen, is ideal ground cover but inclined to be invasive. It has dark green leaves marked with a purple V-shaped band and panicles of pink flowers in summer. Height 3 in (8 cm), spread 36 in (90 cm). *P. vacciniifolia* (zones 7-9) is a semi-evergreen, creeping plant with glossy, mid-green leaves that turn red in autumn. The flowers are produced in long spikes of deep pink in summer and autumn. Height 10 in (25 cm), spread 24 in (60 cm).

Petasites fragrans (zones 7-9)
Winter heliotrope is a spreading perennial with fleshy rhizomes and kidney-shaped, pale green leaves. The panicles of lilac or purple flowers are strongly scented of vanilla and appear from mid-winter to early spring. Height 12 in (30 cm), spread 5 ft (1.5 m).

Phlox
Phlox bifida (zones 4-8) is a mound-forming evergreen with very thin hairy leaves and fragrant, white to lavender blue flowers in spring and early summer. Height 8 in (20 cm), spread 6 in (15 cm). *P. divaricata* (wild sweet William) (zones 4-8) is a spreading, semi-evergreen with hairy, mid-green leaves. It flowers in early summer in a range of colors from white through lavender blue to violet. Height 16 in (40 cm), spread 24 in (60 cm).

Phlox douglasii (zones 5-7), also a mound-forming evergreen, has small, dark green leaves, produces pale blue or pink flowers in late spring and early summer. Height 8 in (20 cm), spread 12 in (30 cm). *P. nana* (Santa Fé phlox) (zones 7-8), deciduous and spreading by runners, has downy, gray-green leaves. It flowers from summer to autumn in a range of colors from white to pink and purple. Height 8 in (20 cm), spread 12 in (30 cm) *P. subulata* (zones 3-8), a dense evergreen with bright green, hairy leaves, flowers in late spring and early summer in a range of colors including white, pink, lilac, purple and red. Height 6 in (15 cm), spread 24 in (60 cm).

Polemonium (zones 4-8)
Polemonium 'Lambrook Mauve' forms a rounded mound with pinnate, dark green leaves and bell-shaped lilac blue flowers in late spring and early summer. Height and

Pulsatilla vulgaris

spread 18 in (45 cm). *P. pulcherrimum* forms clumps with pinnate leaves and bell-shaped white, light blue or dark blue flowers in early summer. Height and spread 12 in (30 cm).

Polygala calcarea (zones 7-9)
Milkwort is a prostrate, creeping, evergreen with leathery, mid-green leaves. Royal blue flowers have white tips to the lower petals in late spring and early summer. Height 2 in (5 cm), spread 8 in (20 cm). The variety *P. c.* 'Lillet' has bright blue flowers.

Potentilla
Potentilla alba (zones 5-8) is a clump-former with pale green leaves, silver beneath, and large white flowers in late spring and early summer. Height 4 in (10 cm), spread 12 in (30 cm). *P. eriocarpa* (zones 6-8), a carpeting perennial, has bright green leaves and large, deep yellow flowers in early summer. Height 4 in (10 cm), spread 12 in (30 cm). *P.* 'William Rollison' (zones 5-8), a clump-former, has mid-green leaves and semi-double yellow or orange flowers with a yellow center in summer. Height 18 in (45 cm), spread 24 in (60 cm).

Primula
Primula auricula (zones 3-7) is a rosette-forming evergreen with pale green or gray-green leaves and umbels of deep yellow fragrant flowers in spring. Height and spread 10 in (20 cm). *P. bulleyana* (zones 5-8), a semi-evergreen Candelabra primula, has rosettes of mid-green leaves and whorls of deep red flowers fading to orange. Height and spread 24 in (60 cm).

Primula hirsuta (zones 3-8) is an evergreen with a rosette of hairy, mid-green leaves and short-stemmed umbels of mauve-pink flowers with a white eye in late spring and early summer. Height 4 in (10 cm), spread 12 in (30 cm). *P. luteola* (zones 5-8), also evergreen, has a rosette of mid-green leaves and umbels of bright yellow flowers in spring. Height 12 in (30 cm), spread 18 in (45 cm).

Primula vulgaris (primrose) (zones 4-7) is a rosette-forming perennial with bright green leaves and pale yellow flowers in late winter and early spring. Height 8 in (20 cm), spread 16 in (40 cm).

Prunella grandiflora (zones 5-8)
Self-heal is a vigorous, spreading perennial with dark green leaves and purple flowers on leafy stems in summer. Height 6 in (15 cm), spread 36 in (90 cm). The variety *P. g.* 'White Loveliness' produces white flowers.

Pterocephalus perennis (zones 5-7)
Evergreen carpet-former with hairy, gray-green leaves and deep pink flower heads in summer. The blooms are followed by papery seed heads. Height 4 in (10 cm), spread 8 in (20 cm).

Pulmonaria
Pulmonaria angustifolia (blue cowslip) (zones 4-8) is a clump-forming perennial, deciduous except in mild areas, with plain, dark green leaves and deep blue flowers in spring. Height 12 in (30 cm), spread 18 in (45 cm). The variety 'Beth's Pink' has white-spotted, dark green leaves and deep pink flowers.

Pulmonaria longifolia (zones 5-8) is deciduous, spreading by rhizomes, with dark green leaves spotted silvery white. Funnel-shaped, deep blue flowers appear in late winter and spring. Height 12 in (30 cm), spread 18 in (45 cm).

Pulmonaria officinalis (spotted dog, Jerusalem cowslip, soldiers and sailors) (zones 5-8) is an evergreen with mid-green, bristly leaves spotted white and flowers that open pink, ageing to violet and finally blue. Height 8 in (20 cm), spread 18 in (45 cm). The variety 'Sissinghurst White' has white flowers, pink in bud, with long leaves and grows to a height of 12 in (30 cm).

Pulmonaria saccharata (Jerusalem sage) (zones 4-8), a clump-forming evergreen, has mid-green, white-spotted leaves. The flowers are red-purple, violet or white appearing from late winter through until late spring. Height 12 in (30 cm), spread 24 in (60 cm).

Pulsatilla vulgaris (zones 5-7)
Pasque flower forms clumps of light green leaves and upright, bell-shaped, silky-hairy flowers that are usually deep purple, occasionally paler or even white. Height and

Potentilla 'William Rollison'

spread 8 in (20 cm).

Pyrola rotundifolia (zones 5-8)
Wintergreen is a creeping perennial with dark green leaves and racemes of white flowers in summer. Height and spread 8 in (20 cm).

Ranunculus aconitifolius 'Flore Pleno' (zones 5-9)
Bachelor's buttons or fair maids of France is a clump-forming perennial with shiny, dark green leaves and double white flowers in late spring and early summer. Height 24 in (60 cm), spread 18 in (45 cm).

Raoulia australis (zones 8-9)
Prostrate, carpet-forming, with tiny, spoon-shaped, silver-gray leaves and bright yellow flowers in summer. Height 1 in (2 cm), spread 12 in (30 cm).

Saponaria
Saponaria 'Bressingham' (zones 5-8) is carpet-forming with mid-green leaves and a mass of deep pink flowers in summer. Height 4 in (10 cm), spread 12 in (30 cm).

Saponaria ocymoides (zones 4-8), sometimes known as Tumbling Ted, is a quick-spreading, carpet-former with bright green, hairy leaves and bright pink flowers in summer. Height 4 in (10 cm), spread 18 in (45 cm). The variety *S. o.*

'Alba' is slower growing with white flowers.

Saxifraga

Saxifraga 'Bob Hawkins' (zones 6-8) is carpet-forming, with rosettes of light green, white-variegated leaves and greenish white flowers in summer. Height 8 in (20 cm), spread 12 in (30 cm).

S. exarata moschata (zones 5-7) forms a mossy cushion with rosettes of light green leaves and yellow flowers from spring until autumn. Height 4 in (10 cm), spread 12 in (30 cm). *S. e. m.* 'Cloth of Gold' has golden foliage.

Saxifraga marginata (zones 6-7) is carpet-forming and vigorous with lime-encrusted, silver-gray foliage and white flowers in spring. Height 4 in (10 cm), spread 12 in (30 cm). *S.* 'Southside Seedling' also forms a carpet but has pale green leaves and arching panicles of white flowers spotted red in late spring and early summer. Height and spread 12 in (30 cm). *S.* x *urbium* (London pride) (zones 6-7) is a vigorous spreading plant with rosettes of leathery, mid-green leaves and tiny star-shaped, white-flushed pink flowers during summer.

Stachys byzantina

Height 12 in (30 cm), spread indefinite.

Scabiosa graminifolia (zones 4-9)

Evergreen, clump-former with pale green leaves and large lilac flowers in summer. Height and spread 12 in (30 cm).

Sedum

Sedum acre (common stonecrop) (zones 4-9) is a carpet-forming evergreen with pale green leaves and sheets of star-shaped, green-yellow flowers all summer. Height 2 in (5 cm), spread 24 in (60 cm). *S. lydium* (zones 5-8) is similar in habit but has tight rosettes of mid-green, red-tipped leaves and small star-shaped, white flowers in summer. Height 2 in (5 cm), spread 10 in (25 cm).

Shortia galacifolia (zones 6-9)

Clump-former whose shiny, dark green leaves turn red in autumn. Large, funnel-shaped white flowers are flushed pink in late spring. Height 6 in (15 cm), spread 12 in (30 cm).

Silene schafta (zones 5-7)

Clump-forming semi-evergreen with bright green leaves and deep cerise flowers, opening star-shaped on long tubes during late summer and autumn. Height and spread 8 in (20 cm).

Stachys byzantina (zones 4-8)

Lamb's ears is carpet-forming, with wrinkled gray-green leaves and woolly spikes of deep pink flowers in summer and early autumn. Height 18 in (45 cm), spread 24 in (60 cm). The variety *S. b* 'Silver Carpet' has gray-green leaves and is non-flowering.

Symphytum (zones 5-9)

Symphytum 'Goldsmith' forms clumps of dark green leaves with gold and cream blotches and light blue, pink or cream flowers in spring. Height and spread 12 in (30 cm). *S. ibericum* is hairy with large, light green leaves and pale yellow flowers in late spring and early summer. Height 18 in (45 cm), spread 36 in (90 cm)

Tanakaea radicans (zones 6-8)

Japanese foam flower is a dense evergreen

with leathery leaves, dark green above pale green on the underside. The star-shaped white flowers are held in large panicles during spring and early summer. Height 4 in (10 cm), spread 12 in (30 cm).

Tellima grandiflora 'Perky' (zones 4-8)

Rosette-forming with hairy, mid-green, heart- or kidney-shaped leaves and red flowers Height 18 in (45 cm), spread 12 in (30 cm).

Tiarella cordifolia (zones 3-7)

Foam flower is a vigorous plant, spreading by stolons, with pale green leaves turning deep red in autumn and racemes of small creamy white flowers in summer. Height and spread 12 in (30 cm).

Tolmiea menziesii (zones 6-9)

Piggy-back plant is a fast-spreader whose lime green leaves have prominent veins. Produces young plants where the leaf stalk and blade meet. The flowers have light green sepals, brown petals and orange anthers with a slight scent in spring and early summer. Height 24 in (60 cm), spread 6 ft 6 in (2 m).

Tradescantia Andersoniana Group (zones 5-9)

Clump-forming evergreen with mid-green, fleshy leaves, sometimes tinted purple. White, pink, purple or blue flowers appear in late spring and early summer. Height 18 in (45 cm), spread 24 in (60 cm).

Tricyrtis flava (zones 6-9)

Clump-forming, with mid-green leaves and purple spots. Star-shaped yellow flowers with brownish purple spots appear from the leaf axils in autumn. Height and spread 12 in (30 cm).

Trifolium

Trifolium pratense 'Susan Smith' (zones 6-9) is carpet-forming, with mid-green leaves etched with fine gold lines. Pink flowers appear in early summer. Height 6 in (15 cm), spread 18 in (45 cm). The vigorous *T. repens* 'Purpurascens Quadrifolium' (zones 4-8) has crimson-purple leaves edged with light green and small white flowers in summer. Height 4

Veronica spicata

in (10 cm), spread indefinite.

Verbena 'Sissinghurst' (zones 7-11)
Carpet-forming, with dark green leaves and magenta-pink flowers in summer. Height 8 in (20 cm), spread 36 in (90 cm).

Veronica
Veronica gentianoides (zones 4-7) is carpet-forming, with thick, dark green leaves and terminal racemes of pale blue or white flowers in early summer. Height and spread 20 in (50 cm). *V. spicata* (zones 3-8) has pale green, hairy leaves and bright blue flowers with purple stamens in spring and summer. Height 12 in (30 cm), spread 18 in (45 cm).

Viola
Viola cornuta (horned violet) (zones 7-9) is a spreading evergreen with mid-green leaves. The flowers, produced during spring and summer, are lilac-blue with a slight scent. Height 6 in (15 cm), spread 20 in (50 cm). *V.* 'Jackanapes' (zones 4-8) is fast-growing with bright green leaves. Its lovely flowers are produced in spring and summer. They have deep purple-brown top petals and lower petals that are golden yellow streaked with purple towards the center. Height 4 in (10 cm), spread 12 in (30 cm).

Waldsteinia ternata (zones 3-8)
Fast-growing semi-evergreen with mid-green leaves and bright yellow flowers in late spring and early summer. Height 4 in

(10 cm), spread 36 in (90 cm).

MEDIUM-GROWING

Achillea ptarmica 'The Pearl' (zones 3-8)
Upright perennial that spreads rapidly, with shiny, dark green leaves and masses of small, button-like white flowers in summer. Height and spread 30 in (75 cm).

Aciphylla aurea (zones 8-10)
Golden Spaniard is a rosette-forming ever-green with bayonet-shaped yellow-green leaves and a 6 ft 6 in (2 m) spike of lots of small golden yellow flowers in spring and early summer. Height and spread 32 in (80 cm).

Aconitum anthora (zones 5-8)
Upright with dark green leaves and deep blue or pale yellow racemes of bloom in late summer. Height 30 in (75 cm), spread 12 in (30 cm).

Agapanthus (zones 7-10)
Agapanthus campanulatus is vigorous, clump-forming and deciduous, with strap-like gray-green leaves and umbels of bell-shaped pale or dark blue flowers on long stems in mid-to late summer. Height 3 ft (1 m), spread 18 in (45 cm). *A.* 'Dorothy Palmer' also forms clumps. It has strap-like leaves and trumpet-shaped, deep blue flowers turning mauve in late summer. Height 36 in (90 cm), spread 24 in (60 cm).

Althaea armeniaca (zones 3-9)
Erect perennial with dark green leaves paler on the underside. Racemes of funnel-shaped, deep pink flowers appear from the leaf axils in summer and early autumn. Height 4 ft (1.2 m), spread 12 in (30 cm).

Amsonia illustrus (zones 5-9)
Clump-forming, with glossy, bright green leaves and panicles of light blue flowers in late spring and early summer. Height 4 ft (1.2 m), spread 18 in (45 cm).

Anchusa azurea/Anchusa italica (zones 3-8)
Erect and clump-forming, with dark green, hairy leaves and bright blue flowers that age to purple in large panicles in early summer.

Height 40 in (1 m), spread 24 in (60 cm).

Anemone
Anemone hupehensis (zones 4-8) is an erect perennial spreading by suckers, with dark green basal leaves and pink or white flowers on long stems in late summer. Height 36 in (90 cm), spread 18 in (45 cm). *A.* x *hybrida* (Japanese anemone) (zones 4-8) is more vigorous, also spreading by suckers, with mid-green leaves, hairy on the underside. The flowers appear from late summer through to late autumn and are semi-double, deep pink, on long branched stems. Height 4 ft (1.2 m), spread indefinite. *A. rivularis* (zones 6-8) forms clumps of dark green leaves and white flowers on long branching stems. The reverse of the petals (properly called tepals since they are neither petals nor sepals) is often an attractive blue color. The flowers are produced in late spring and early summer with another flush in autumn. Height 36 in (90 cm), spread 12 in (30 cm).

Aquilegia chrysantha (zones 3-8)
Vigorous with mid-green leaves and flowers with golden yellow sepals and pale yellow petals appearing in late spring and early summer. Height 36 in (90 cm), spread 24 in (60 cm).

Aruncus dioicus 'Kneiffii' (zones 3-7)
Goatsbeard is hummock-forming with finely divided, mid-green, fern-like leaves and masses of tiny cream flowers on arching stems in summer. Take the time to remove

Aciphylla aurea

the dead flower stems because, as with so many other white-flowered plants the brown faded blooms are unsightly. Height 4 ft (1.2 m), spread 18 in (45 cm).

Aster (zones 4-8)

Aster novae-angliae (New England aster) is clump-forming with mid-green leaves and woody stems carrying daisy-like blue-purple flowers with yellow central disc florets in late summer and autumn. Height 5 ft (1.5 m), spread 24 in (60 cm). *A. novi-belgii* (Michaelmas daisy, New York aster) has mid-green leaves and violet flowers with yellow central disc florets. Height 4 ft (1.2 m), spread 36 in (90 cm).

Astilbe (zones 4-9)

Astilbe 'Professor van der Wielen' is clump-forming with mid-green leaves and arching plumes of white flowers in summer. Height 4 ft (1.2 m), spread 36 in (90cm). *A.* 'Straussenfeder' (ostrich plume) is vigorous with bronze-tinted young foliage becoming mid-green in summer. The flowers are rosy pink, borne in loose arching sprays in summer and autumn. Height 36 in (90 cm), spread 24 in (60 cm).

Baptista australis (zones 3-9)

False indigo is upright with bright green leaves and pea-like deep blue flowers in summer. Its dark green seed pods are good for flower arranging. Height 32 in (80 cm), spread 24 in (60 cm).

Campanula

Campanula latifolia (zones 4-8) is vigorous, with mid-green leaves and bell-shaped white, pale or deep blue flowers from the leaf axils in summer. Height 4 ft (1.2 m), spread 24 in (60 cm). *C. persicifolia* (zones 3-8) is evergreen, forming rosettes with bright green basal leaves and white to mid-blue, pendant, cup-shaped flowers in midsummer. Height 36 in (90 cm),

Left *Agapanthus campanulatus* against a backdrop of *Phormium* (the New Zealand flax), hydrangea, *Musa* (banana plant) and *Brachycome iberidifolia* (Swan River daisy).

Centaurea cineraria 'Colchester'

spread 12 in (30 cm).

Cardamine raphanifolia (zones 3-9)

Dark green leaves and lilac flowers in early summer. Height 36 in (90 cm), spread 24 in (60 cm).

Caulophyllum thalictroides (zones 3-8)

Rhizomatous with mid-green leaves and yellow-brown flowers in late spring, followed by bright blue seeds. Height 30 in (75 cm), spread 10 in (25 cm).

Centaurea

Centaurea cinerarea (zones 7-9) is an evergreen with gray leaves and purple flowers in summer. Height 36 in (90 cm), spread 18 in (45 cm). *C. macrocephala* (zones 3-7) is a strong-growing clump-former with mid-green leaves and bright yellow, thistle-like flowers with shiny brown bracts in summer. Height 5 ft (1.5 m), spread 24 in (60 cm).

Centranthus ruber (zones 5-8)

Red valerian is clump-forming with fleshy mid-green leaves and fragrant white, pale pink or deep red funnel-shaped flowers in late spring through until late autumn. Height and spread 36 in (90 cm).

Cimicifuga

Cimicifuga japonica (zones 4-7) is clump-forming with deep green leaves and racemes of

pure white flowers in late summer and autumn. Height 36 in (90 cm), spread 24 in (60 cm). *C. racemosa* (black snake root) (zones 3-7) has dark green leaves and white flowers in mid-summer, but, it has the most awful smell. Height 4 ft (1.2 m), spread 24 in (60 cm).

Clematis (zones 3-7)

Clematis integrifolia has mid-green leaves and bell-shaped, purple-blue flowers with twisted sepals and pale yellow anthers in summer. The flowers are followed by silvery seed heads. Height 36 in (90 cm), spread 24 in (60 cm). *C. recta* is a clump-former with gray foliage and star-shaped white flowers with cream anthers in autumn. The flowers have a wonderful fragrance and are followed by gray seed heads. Height 36 in (90 cm), spread 32 in (80 cm).

Coreopsis (zones 4-9)

Coreopsis auriculata has mid-green leaves and large bright yellow flowers in early and mid-summer. Height 36 in (90 cm), spread 24 in (60 cm). *C. verticifolia* is a spreader with mid-green leaves and bright yellow flowers in early summer. Height 24 in (90 cm), spread 24 in (60 cm).

Corydalis nobilis (zones 5-8)

Strong-growing, with dark blue-green leaves and racemes of pale yellow flowers, each with a brown spot and a short dark yellow spur. Height 32 in (80 cm), spread 18 in (45 cm).

Digitalis laevigata (zones 7-9)

Clump-forming, with mid-green basal leaves and dull fawn-yellow flowers with a white lip. In summer it has freckles inside the bloom. Height 36 in (90 cm), spread 18 in (45 cm).

Disporum hookeri (zones 4-9)

Mid-green leaves and bell-shaped creamy green flowers in spring, followed by orange-red berries. Height 36 in (90 cm), spread 18 in (45 cm).

Doronicum

Doronicum austriacum (zones 5-8) is clump-forming, with hairy, mid-green basal leaves and bright yellow, daisy-like flowers in late spring and early summer. Height and spread 4 ft (1.2 m). *D. pardalianches* (zones 4-8) has pale yellow flowers on long stems in late spring and early summer. Height and spread 36 in (90 cm).

Echinacea angustifolia (zones 4-9)
Erect with mid-green leaves and large, daisy like, early summer flowers, that are pink with an orange-brown conical disc. Height 36 in (90 cm), spread 18 in (45 cm).

Echium wildpretii (zones 9-10)
Woody-stemmed, short-lived, tender perennial, succeeding only in a sheltered, sunny position. It has a rosette of lance-shaped, light, silvery green leaves and a dense spike of small, funnel-shaped red flowers. Height 5 ft (1.5 m), spread 24 in (60 cm).

Epilobium angustifolium (zones 3-7)
Vigorous spreader with willow-like, pale green leaves and open white flowers with green sepals in summer and early autumn. A few words of warning: this is a form of

Echium wildpretii

willow herb, a weed by any other name and it will self-seed readily. Height 5 ft (1.5 m), spread 36 in (90 cm).

Eryngium
Eryngium alpinum (sea holly) (zones 5-8) is a rosette-forming perennial with mid-green leaves. Steel-blue flowers with soft spiny bracts on blue stems appear during summer and early autumn. Height 36 in (90 cm), spread 18 in (45 cm). The evergreen, clump-forming *E. planum* (zones 5-9) has dark green basal leaves and light blue flowers with spiny blue-green bracts in late summer and early autumn. Height 36 in (90 cm), spread 18 in (45 cm).

Erysimum 'Bowles' Mauve' (zones 6-10)
Fast-growing evergreen with gray-green leaves and mauve flowers. These are produced mainly from winter through to summer, but can appear all year long. Height 32 in (80 cm), spread 24 in (60 cm).

Eupatorium cannabinum (zones 3-9)
Strong grower with dark green leaves and panicles of white, pink or purple flowers in late summer and early autumn. Height and spread 4 ft (1.2 m).

Euphorbia
Euphorbia amygdaloides (wood spurge) (zones 6-9) is an evergreen with dull, dark green leaves that are red-brown underneath. Greenish yellow flowers appear during late spring and early summer. Height 30 in (75 cm), spread 12 in (30 cm). The variety *E. a. robbiae* (zones 6-9) has dark green, leathery leaves spreading by rhizomes and can become invasive.

Euphorbia griffithii (zones 4-9) has dark green leaves with red mid-ribs and orange bracts with bright yellow centers in early summer. Can be invasive, reaches a height 36 in (90 cm) and spread of 24 in (60 cm).

Filipendula (zones 3-9)
Filipendula palmata is clump-forming, with large mid-green leaves woolly-white on the underside and masses of pale pink, feathery flowers in summer. Height 3 ft (1 m), spread

Gaillardia x grandiflora 'Burgundy'

24 in (60 cm). *F. rubra* (queen of the prairies) is a large spreader with mid-green leaves and deep pink, sweetly fragrant flowers on deep red stems in early summer. Height 6 ft (1.8 m), spread 4 ft (1.2 m).

Gaillardia x grandiflora (zones 3-8)
Blanket flower is a short-lived perennial with gray-green leaves. Yellow ray florets and brown-yellow disc florets are borne on short stems in summer and early autumn. Height 36 in (90 cm), spread 18 in (45 cm).

Gaura lindheimeri (zones 6-9)
Clump-former with thin mid-green leaves and pink flower buds from early summer until early autumn. These open at dawn and are pure white fading to a pinkish white. Height 4 ft (1.2 m), spread 36 in (90 cm).

Gentiana asclepiadea (zones 6-9)
Willow gentian is a clump-former with mid-green leaves and clusters of trumpet-shaped, dark blue flowers in early summer through to autumn. Height 32 in (80 cm), spread 18 in (45 cm). The variety *G. a.* 'Alba' has white flowers with a green tinge.

Geranium
Geranium maderense (zones 8-9) is a strong-growing, evergreen with very large bright

green leaves and red stalks. The flowers appear from late winter until late summer and are magenta-pink, with deeper pink veins, on long multiple stems above the leaves. Height and spread 4 ft (1.2 m). Unfortunately this is not a hardy species and will succeed only in a warm, sheltered position.

Geranium phaeum (mourning widow) (zones 4-8) is a clump-former with pale green, brown-marked leaves. The flowers, in late spring and early summer, range from white through pink, blue, mauve, violet and maroon to almost black, most with a white center. Height 36 in (90 cm), spread 18 in (45 cm).

Geranium psilostemon (Armenian cranesbill) (zones 5-8) also forms clumps, with mid-green leaves shaded magenta in spring, turning red in autumn. It bears masses of bright, magenta flowers with black centers in summer. Height 36 in (90 cm), spread 24 in (60 cm).

Hedysarum coronarium (zones 4-9)
French honeysuckle is an upright, dense perennial with mid-green leaves and racemes of fragrant, deep red flowers on long stems in spring. Height and spread 36 in (90 cm).

Helenium 'Bressingham Gold' (zones 4-8)
Vigorous clump-former with mid-green

Hedysarum coronarium

leaves and large flowers of gold ray florets shaded crimson and brown disc florets in mid-summer and early autumn. Height 36 in (90 cm), spread 24 in (60 cm).

Helianthus x multiflorus (zones 5-9)
Clump-forming, with dark green leaves. Golden ray florets and deep yellow-brown disc florets appear in late summer and autumn. Height 5 ft (1.5 m), spread 36 in (90 cm). The variety *H x m.* 'Loddon Gold' has double, bright yellow flowers.

Heliopsis helianthoides (zones 4-9)
Clump-former with mid-green leaves and single or double bright yellow flowers on long stalks in mid-summer and early autumn. Height 5 ft (1.5 m), spread 24 in (60 cm). The variety *H. h.* 'Light of Loddon' has semi-double bright golden flowers with dark green leaves and grows to 40 in (1 m).

Helleborus foetidus (zones 6-9)
Stinking hellebore is an erect perennial with dark green leaves that do stink (but only if they are crushed) and bell-shaped, purple-edged, green flowers that are usually fragrant, with pale green bracts. Flowers are produced from mid-winter until late spring. Height 28 in (70 cm), spread 18 in (45 cm).

Hemerocallis (zones 3-9)
Hemerocallis 'Aquamarine' (day lily) is an evergreen with strap-like leaves and star-shaped pale blue flowers in early summer. Height 32 in (80 cm), spread 24 in (60 cm). *H.* 'Catherine Woodbery' has pale pink flowers with a light green throat. It flowers over a long period from mid- to late summer. Height 32 in (80 cm), spread 24 in (60 cm).

Hesperis matronalis (zones 4-9)
Sweet rocket forms rosettes of dark green leaves and panicles of purple or sometimes white or lilac flowers in late spring and summer. Height 36 in (90 cm), spread 18 in (45 cm).

Heuchera 'Green Ivory' (zones 4-8)
Clump-former with dark green leaves and

Helianthus x *multiflorus* 'Loddon Gold'

panicles of small green flowers on stiff stems in early summer. Height and spread 32 in (80 cm).

Hosta (zones 3-9)
Hosta 'Blue Umbrellas' is a clump-former with large, stiff, thick, blue-green leaves and bell-shaped dirty white flowers on long stems in mid-summer. Height and spread 36 in (90 cm).

H. opipara has shiny, bright green, leathery leaves with creamy yellow margins and bell-shaped, mauve flowers with purple stripes in late summer. Height 32 in (80 cm), spread 5 ft (1.5 m).

Inula helenium (zones 5-8)
Strong grower with long, mid-green leaves, woolly underneath, and bright yellow flowers in mid-to late summer. Height and spread 36 in (90 cm).

Isatis tinctoria (zones 4-8)
Woad is a short-lived perennial with gray-green leaves and panicles of yellow flowers in summer. The leaves produce a blue pigment when fermented with ammonia but, I warn you, it self-seeds all over the place. Height 3 ft (1 m), spread 18 in (45 cm).

Kirengeshoma palmata (zones 5-8)
Clump-former with pale green leaves on purple, arching stems and tubular, pale yellow flowers in late summer and early autumn.

Height 3 ft (1 m), spread 32 in (80 cm).

Kniphofia (zones 6-9)

Kniphofia 'Atlanta' (torch lily or red hot poker) is an evergreen with strap-like gray-green leaves and orange-red flowers fading to pale yellow in late spring and early summer. Height 4 ft (1.2 m), spread 36 in (90 cm).

Kniphofia ensifolia is a strong-growing evergreen with arching, blue-green leaves and pale green-white flowers, red in the bud stage in late summer and early autumn. Height 4 ft (1.2 m), spread 24 in (60 cm).

Kniphofia northiae, also evergreen, does not form clumps. It has long, broad glaucous leaves and dense racemes of pale yellow flowers in summer. Height 5 ft (1.5 m), spread 36 in (90 cm).

Lathyrus gmelinii (zones 6-9)

Everlasting pea is a clump-former with mid-green leaves. Orange-yellow flowers with brown stripes appear from spring to mid-summer. Height 36 in (90 cm), spread 12 in (30 cm)

Lavatera maritima (zones 6-8)

Shrubby evergreen with gray-green leaves and single, saucer-shaped, white, pink or deep pink flowers with magenta veins in late summer and autumn. Height 5 ft (1.5 m), spread 3 ft (90 cm).

Leucanthemum x superbum (zones 5-8)

Shasta daisy is a strong-growing clump-former with glossy, dark green, basal leaves and single or double flowers with yellow disc florets from early summer to early autumn. Height 36 in (90 cm), spread 24 in (60 cm).

Libertia grandiflora (zones 8-10)

Evergreen with dense clumps of long, dark green, leathery leaves and long panicles of white flowers with brown outer lower petals in late spring and early summer. Height 36 in (90 cm), spread 24 in (60 cm).

Ligularia dentata (zones 4-8)

Clump-former with large, mid-green, basal leaves with red stalks and large orange-yellow daisy-like flowers with brown centers in summer and early autumn. Height and spread 40 in (1 m). The variety *L. d.* 'Desdemona' has brown-green leaves that are purple-maroon on the underside.

Lobelia (zones 4-9)

Lobelia 'Bees' Flame' is a clump-former with red-purple leaves and stems and racemes of bright crimson flowers in mid- to late summer. Height 32 in (80 cm), spread 12 in (30 cm).

Lobelia cardinalis (cardinal flower) (zones 3-9) is similar in habit with shiny, deep green, bronze-tinged leaves and tubular scarlet flowers with purple bracts in summer and autumn. Height 36 in (90 cm), spread 12 in (30 cm).

Lunaria rediviva (zones 6-9)

Honesty forms clumps of dark green leaves and fragrant, pink-white flowers in late spring and early summer. The flowers are followed by flat, beige, elliptic seed pods. Height 36 in (90 cm), spread 12 in (30 cm).

Lupinus 'Thundercloud' (zones 5-8)

Clump-former with mid-green leaves and racemes of deep blue flowers in summer. Height and spread 36 in (90 cm).

Lychnis flos-cuculi (zones 6-9)

Ragged robin is a spreading perennial with blue-green leaves and star-shaped, pink or purple-pink flowers in late spring and early summer. Height and spread 36 in (90 cm).

Lysimachia

Lysimachia ciliata (zones 3-9) has hairy mid-green leaves and star-shaped, yellow flowers with red-brown centers in summer. Height 4 ft (1.2 m), spread 24 in (60 cm). *L. punctata* (zones 4-8) is liable to be invasive. It has dark green leaves and whorls of cup-shaped, bright yellow flowers in late summer. Height 36 in (90 cm), spread 24 in (60 cm). *L. vulgaris* (yellow loosestrife) (zones 5-9) spreads by stolons and has mid-green leaves and terminal panicles of bright yellow flowers in summer. Height and spread 4 ft (1.2 m).

Lythrum virgatum (zones 4-9)

Clump-former with dark green leaves and racemes of star-shaped, deep red flowers in summer. Height 36 in (90 cm), spread

Lythrum virgatum 'The Rocket'

18 in (45 cm).

Macleaya microcarpa 'Kelway's Coral Plume' (zones 4-9)
Dark, gray-green leaves, white on the underside, and large panicles of coral pink flowers, deep pink in bud, in summer. Height 6 ft (1.8 m), spread 4 ft (1.2 m).

Meconopsis paniculata (zones 8-9)
Evergreen monocarpic perennial (that is, dying after it flowers and forms seed) with rosettes of long gray-green leaves covered with yellow hairs and racemes of cup-shaped, pale yellow flowers in late spring and early summer. Height 6 ft (2 m), spread 24 in (60 cm).

Mimulus ringens (zones 3-7)
Monkey flower is an erect perennial with square stems and mid-green leaves and single white or violet flowers in summer. Height 36 in (90 cm), spread 12 in (30 cm).

Monarda (zones 4-9)
The two most useful ground-covering species of bergamot are both clump-formers with a height of 36 in (90 cm) leaves and single, white flowers with golden yellow stamens, two to a stem, in late spring. Height and spread 24 in (60 cm).

Morina persica (zones 5-9)
Rosette-forming evergreen with spiny, dark green, basal leaves and masses of whorled clusters of white fragrant flowers that turn deep pink after fertilization. Height 4 ft (1.2 m), spread to 24 in (60 cm).

Nepeta sibirica (zones 3-8)
Erect perennial with dark green aromatic leaves and lavender blue flowers in summer. Height 36 in (90 cm), spread 18 in (45 cm).

Paeonia
Paeonia 'Dresden' (zones 3-8) is a vigorous herbaceous perennial with deep green leaves that turn crimson in autumn and large, single, white flowers, flushed pink in summer. Height and spread 36 in (90 cm). *P. emodi* (Himalayan peony) (zones 6-8) is less

Papaver orientale 'Turkishi'

vigorous, with dark green leaves and single, white flowers with golden yellow stamens, two to a stem, in late spring. Height and spread 24 in (60 cm).

Paeonia mascula (zones 5-8) is an erect perennial with blue-green leaves, pale green on the underside and bowl-shaped, single, deep red flowers with golden yellow stamens in summer. Also erect, *P. mlokosewitschii* (Molly the witch) (zones 4-8) has blue-green leaves, paler underneath, and single, bowl-shaped, bright yellow flowers with pale yellow stamens in late spring and early summer. Height and spread of both these species 36 in (90 cm).

Papaver orientale (zones 4-9)
Oriental poppy is a clump-former with mid-green leaves. The cup-shaped orange-red flowers appear in late spring and early summer with a black blotch at the base of each petal. Height and spread 36 in (90 cm).

Parahebe perfoliata (zones 9-10)
Digger's speedwell is an evergreen with gray-green leaves, each pair at right angles to the pair below. Racemes of blue flowers appear in mid-summer. Height 24 in (60 cm), spread 18 in (45 cm).

Paris polyphilla (zones 5-8)
A spreader with mid-green leaves and spider-like flowers with yellow-green inner petals and green outer petals in summer followed by green seed pods that open when

ripe to display bright red seeds. Height 3 ft (1 m), spread 12 in (30 cm).

Penstemon digitalis (zones 2-8)
Semi-evergreen, vigorous perennial with purple stems and mid-green leaves. The panicles of white, bell-shaped flowers, sometimes tinged with pink, in summer. Height 36 in (90 cm), spread 18 in (45 cm).

Persicaria amplexicaulis (zones 5-8)
Strong-growing semi-evergreen with mid-green leaves and spikes of white or bright red flowers in summer and early autumn. Height and spread 4 ft (1.2 m).

Petasites japonicus (zones 5-9)
An invasive weed of a perennial that spreads at an amazing rate and has mid-green leaves up to 3 ft (1 m) in size. The clusters of yellowish green flowers are produced in winter and early spring, before the leaves. Height 36 in (90 cm), spread 5 ft (1.5 m).

Phlox carolina (zones 5-8)
Thick-leafed phlox is a spreading herbaceous perennial with thick, mid-green leaves and

Petasites japonicus

pink, lavender or purple flowers in summer. Height 4 ft (1.2 m), spread 18 in (45 cm).

Physalis alkekengi (zones 5-8)
Chinese lantern is a vigorous spreader with bright green leaves and bell-shaped, cream flowers from the leaf axils in mid-summer followed by bright red berries enclosed in scarlet, papery calyces. Height 24 in (60 cm), spread 3 ft (1 m).

Phytolacca americana (zones 5-9)
Pokeweed or red ink plant is an erect perennial with red stems and large mid-green leaves that are purple-tinged in late summer. Racemes of pink flowers in summer are followed by deep maroon, almost black berries in late autumn. Height 10 ft (3 m), spread 3 ft (1 m).

Pimpinella major (zones 5-8)
Erect perennial with mid-green leaves and umbels of green-white or pink flowers in late spring. Height 4 ft (1.2 m), spread 32 in (80 cm).

Polygonatum
Polygonatum x *hybridum* (Solomon's seal) (zones 6-9) has mid-green leaves and pendant cream flowers with green tips in late spring, followed by blue-black fruit. Height 4 ft (1.2 m), spread 18 in (45 cm). *P. multiflorum* (zones 4-8) has arching stems of mid-green leaves and clusters of white flowers with green tips at the leaf axils in late spring, followed by black fruit. Height 36 in (90 cm), spread 12 in (30 cm). The variety *P. m.* 'Striatum' has mid-green leaves striped creamy white.

Potentilla atrosanguinea (zones 5-8)
Clump-former with gray, hairy leaves and yellow, orange or red saucer-shaped flowers in summer and autumn. Height 36 in (90 cm), spread 24 in (60 cm).

Primula florindae (zones 3-8)
Giant cowslip is deciduous with mid-green leaves and fragrant yellow tubular flowers in clusters on long stems in early summer. Height 4 ft (1.2 m), spread 36 in (90cm).

Ranunculus lyalli (zones 6-7)
Giant buttercup or Mount Cook lily is semi-evergreen with leathery, dark green, basal leaves and panicles of cup-shaped white flowers in summer. Height 36 in (90 cm), spread 18 in (45 cm).

Rodgersia pinnata and *Rodgersia aesculifolia* growing among *Trollius* and *Lilium*

Rheum palmatum (zones 6-9)
Chinese rhubarb has a thick root and stem and large dark green leaves, similar to those of edible rhubarb, but is grown only for its ornamental leaves and flower spike. Tiny, deep red flowers are carried on enormous panicles up to 6 ft 6 in (2 m) high in early summer. Height 8 ft (2.5 m), spread 5 ft (1.5 m).

Rodgersia (zones 5-8)
These are all clump-forming perennials.

Rodgersia pinnata has deep-veined, shiny, dark green leaves and panicles of white, pink or red star-shaped flowers in mid- and late summer. Height 4 ft (1.2 m), spread 32 in (80 cm) The variety. *R. p.* 'Superba' has bright pink flowers and bronze young foliage.

Rodgersia podophylla has glossy, mid-green leaves, bronze when young, and panicles of creamy green, star-shaped flowers in mid-and late summer. Height and spread 5 ft (1.5 m). *R. sambucifolia* has dark green leaves and dense panicles of star-shaped, pink or sometimes white flowers in early to mid- summer. Height and spread 36 in (90 cm).

Sanguisorba canadensis (zones 3-8)
Canadian burnet is a spreading clump-former with hairy, dark green leaves and spikes of green buds that open from the bottom up into white, fluffy flowers in autumn. Height 6 ft 6 in (2 m), spread 3 ft (1 m).

Smilacina racemosa (zones 4-9)
Clump-former with mid-green leaves turning yellow in autumn. Terminal panicles of creamy white flowers appear in late spring, followed by red berries. Height 36 in (90 cm), spread 24 in (60 cm).

Tricyrtis hirta (zones 4-9)
Clump-former with hairy, pale green leaves. Clusters of funnel-shaped white flowers with purple spots and stigmas appear in late summer and autumn. Height and spread 32 in (80 cm).

Right Rheum palmatum

SHRUBS

It is nice to think big and shrubs allow you to do just that. It is easy to provide shrubs to cover the soil surface and there is a wide range to meet all sorts of situations. Rhododendron, Camellia, Mahonia, Viburnum *(some)*, Choisya, Eleagnus, Ceanothus, Aucuba, Escallonia, Kalmia, Osmanthus *and* Senecio *are all evergreen and only represent a fraction of those that come to mind. Deciduous shrubs include* Viburnum, Rosa, Hydrangea, Magnolia, Philadelphus, Forsythia, Cotinus, Weigela *and* Corylus. *The list is endless (I hope not or I will have to call this book 'Ground Cover ad infinitum').*

Shrubs are easy to grow and if well looked after will provide years of satisfaction. Check the ultimate height and spread of the plant and position it far enough away from its neighbours to prevent competition and overcrowding. If plants have been positioned closely for immediate effect, thin them out and remove the surplus as soon as they meet in the bed.

Please, please, please don't impulse buy plants. All too often a plant is purchased when it is in flower and has instant appeal, but the purchaser has no particular site in mind. The plant is then put in somewhere 'temporarily', until the right spot can be found, and remains there forever, a permanent 'temporary' plant. Far better to take a walk round your garden, find a nice space, large or small, and then go to the garden center and buy a shrub suited to the chosen site.

For many shrubs, pruning is essential to keep the plant supplied with young growth from the base. The best way to prune a forsythia is to bring armfuls of flowering branches into the house (it flowers on growth made the previous year). To keep the branches of Cornus alba *looking red, cut the stems close to the ground each spring, since new growth has the best color.*

There comes a time when shrubs are past their best, out of shape, too big, woody-stemmed and growing slowly. It's no crime to practise euthanasia on old shrubs and if the thought of the cost of replacement tends to stay your hand and chainsaw, take the time to work out how little the plant cost ten, fifteen or twenty years ago.

Having said that, shrubs are often expected to perform for many years and so the initial soil preparation is very important. You have only one chance to get the basics right so it is worth taking your time, avoiding short cuts and doing things properly. Always make the planting hole at least half as big again as the root area or pot. Loosen the soil in the base of the hole and fork in bone meal or hoof and horn. These are slow-acting organic fertilisers that release their nutrients over a long period. Old farmyard manure or compost mixed with the soil will help retain moisture and encourage good rooting. If peat is being used as humus or as an acid conditioner for lime-hating plants make sure it is well mixed with the soil. Used on its own around root balls it can cause problems. If it dries out it is practically impossible to wet again. The same can happen to shrubs grown in pots of peat-based compost. Soak newly planted shrubs thoroughly around the roots to settle the soil and on warm days spray over the foliage to reduce transpiration through the leaf pores (stomata).

I have divided shrubs into low and medium-growing. Low shrubs will, under normal circumstances, grow to a height of 24 in (60 cm) and medium to more than 24 in (60).

Bruckenthalia spiculifolia

LOW- GROWING

Andromeda (zones 2-6)

Andromeda polifolia (bog rosemary) is a semi-prostrate evergreen with leathery, dark green leaves and pale pink or white flowers in spring and early summer. It enjoys moist, peaty, acid soil conditions. Height 18 in (45 cm), spread 24 in (60 cm). *A. p.* 'Macrophylla' is lower growing, with dark green leaves and larger deep pink and white flowers. Height 6 in (15 cm), spread 12 in (30 cm). *A. p.* 'Nikko' has gray-green leaves, pink flowers and a height and spread of 12 in (30 cm).

Antirrhinum (zones 8-10)

Antirrhinum pulverulentum is a dwarf shrub with hairy, mid-green leaves and creamy-yellow flowers in summer. Height 8 in (20 cm), spread 12 in (30 cm). *A .sempervirens* has sticky, hairy mid-green leaves and white or cream flowers with purple veins in early and mid-summer. Height and spread 8 in (20 cm).

Arctostaphylos

Arctostaphylos hookeri 'Monterey Carpet' (zones 8-9) is an evergreen with glossy, pale green leaves and purple branches. The racemes of pink-white flowers appear in early summer, followed by red fruit. Height 8 in (20 cm), spread 4 ft (1.2 m). *A. pumila* (zones 8-10) has dark green leaves, pink-tinted white flowers in racemes during summer and deep red fruit in autumn. Height 12 in (30 cm), spread 32 in (80 cm). *A. uva-ursi* (common bearberry, kinni-

kinnick) (zones 2-6) has leathery, dark green leaves, pink-tinted white flowers in summer, red fruit in autumn. Height 4 in (10 cm), spread 24 in (60 cm).

Ballota

Ballota acetabulosa (zones 8-9) is a bushy, evergreen sub-shrub with gray-green leaves and white stems and purple-pink flowers with green calyces in summer. Height and spread 30 in (75 cm). *B. pseudodictamnus* (zones 7-9) is a mound-forming evergreen with gray-green leaves and pink-white flowers with pale green calyces in late spring and early summer. Height 18 in (45 cm), spread 24 in (60 cm).

Berberis

Berberis buxifolia 'Pygmaea' (zones 6-9) is a compact, evergreen with shiny, dark green leaves without spines. It seldom produces its pale yellow flowers. Height 12 in (30 cm), spread 18 in (45 cm). *B. candidula* (zones 6-9) is densely evergreen with shiny, dark green leaves, which are white on the underside and spine-tipped. The single flowers, produced in spring, are clear yellow and are followed by purple fruit. Height 24 in (60 cm), spread 4 ft (1.2 m).

Berberis empterifolia (zones 7-9) is an evergreen with spiny, dark green leaves, gray on the underside and deep yellow flowers in late spring followed by black fruit. Height and spread 24 in (60 cm). The dwarf variety *B. thunbergii* 'Atropurpurea Nana' (zones 5-8) is deciduous with red-purple foliage, spiny stems and pale yellow flowers in spring. Height 24 in (60 cm), spread 32 in (80 cm).

Bruckenthalia spiculifolia (zones 6-8)

Spike heath is an evergreen shrub that requires acid soil. The shiny, dark green leaves are held on stiff stems with deep pink, sometimes white, bell-shaped flowers in

Cassiope lycopodioides 'Beatrice Lilley'

late spring and summer. Height and spread 8 in (20 cm).

Cassiope lycopodioides (zones 4-6)

Carpet-forming evergreen with small, dark green leaves and bell-shaped white flowers with red calyces in late spring. Height 4 in (10 cm), spread 12 in (30 cm).

Chamaecytisus purpureus (zones 6-9)

Dense deciduous shrub with dark green leaves and pale pink or deep pink flowers with dark purple throats in early summer. Height 18 in (45 cm), spread 24 in (60 cm).

Cistus

Cistus x *pulverulentus* 'Sunset' (zones 9-10) is a compact evergreen with gray-green leaves and rose pink flowers with yellow centers in summer. Height 24 in (60 cm), spread 36 in (90 cm). *C. salviifolius* 'Prostratus' (zones 8-10) is a low-spreading evergreen shrub with gray-green leaves and white flowers with yellow centers in summer. Height 12 in (30 cm), spread 36 in (90 cm).

Convolvulus cneorum (zones 8-10)

Compact, bushy, evergreen with silver-green, silky leaves and pink buds opening to white flowers with yellow centers from late spring until mid-summer. Height 24 in (60 cm), spread 36 in (90 cm).

Berberis thunbergii 'Atropurpurea Nana'

Cotoneaster

Flat-growing and deciduous, *Cotoneaster adpressus* (zones 5-8) has mid-green leaves that turn red in autumn and white flowers that turn red in late summer. Height 12 in (30 cm), spread 6 ft 6 in (2 m).

The following species are all evergreen. A prostrate plant, *Cotoneaster dammeri* (zones 6-8) has dark green leaves and white flowers, followed by red fruit. Height 8 in (20 cm), spread 6 ft 6 in (2 m). *C.* 'Gnom' is similar, but the fruits are dull red. Height 12 in (30 cm), spread 6 ft 6 in (2 m).

Cotoneaster procumbens (zones 6-8) is flat-growing with dark green leaves and white flowers in summer and red fruit in autumn. Height 4 in (10 cm), spread 6 ft 6 in (2 m).

Cotoneaster 'Skogholm' (zones 6-8) is low-growing, with shiny mid-green leaves and white flowers in spring followed by bright red fruit. Height 24 in (60 cm), spread up to 10 ft (3 m).

Cytisus (zones 6-9)

Cytisus ardoinoi is a low-growing deciduous shrub with mid-green leaves and bright yellow flowers in late spring and early summer. Height and spread 18 in (45 cm).

Cytisus decumbens is prostrate, with similar flowers and pale green, stalkless leaves. Height 12 in (30 cm), spread 36 in (90 cm).

Daphne

All those listed here are evergreen. *Daphne blagayana* (zones 7-9) is prostrate, with dark green, leathery leaves and terminal clusters of deliciously fragrant, creamy white flowers in spring followed by white or pink fruit. Height 18 in (45 cm), spread 36 in (90 cm).

Daphne cneorum (garland flower) (zones 5-7) is flat-growing with dark green leaves and fragrant rose pink, or sometimes pale pink or white, flowers in late spring. Height 8 in (20 cm), spread 6 ft 6 in (2 m).

Daphne collina (zones 7-8) is a dense shrub with shiny mid-green leaves and terminal clusters of fragrant deep pink flowers in late spring and early summer,

followed by orange-red fruit. Height and spread 24 in (60 cm).

Daphne jasminea (zones 7-9) is low-growing with gray-green leaves and fragrant white or cream flowers, sometimes pink-flushed, in late spring and summer. Height and spread 12 in (30 cm).

Deutzia crenata 'Nikko' (zones 5-8)

Compact, deciduous shrub with mid-green leaves turning purple in autumn and panicles of star-shaped white flowers in summer. Height 24 in (60 cm), spread 36 in (90 cm).

Eriogonum umbellatum (zones 4-8)

Carpet-forming evergreen sub-shrub with mid-green leaves white on the underside and umbels of sulphur yellow flowers in mid- and late summer, turning red as they age. Height 12 in (30 cm), spread 36 in (90 cm).

Euonymus fortunei (zones 5-9)

Euonymus fortunei 'Emerald Gaiety' is a compact evergreen with shiny green leaves edged with white. The leaves are tinged with pink in winter. The flowers are insignificant. Height 24 in (60 cm), spread 5 ft (1.5 m). The leaves of *E. f.* 'Emerald 'n' Gold' have bright yellow margins that turn pink in winter. Height 24 in (60 cm), spread 36 in (90 cm).

Felicia amelloides (Annual)

Bushy sub-shrub usually grown as an annual, with deep green leaves and daisy-like deep blue or pale blue flowers in summer and autumn. In the British Isles it will overwinter only in mild, sheltered positions. Height and spread 24 in (60 cm).

Forsythia viridissima 'Bronxensis' (zones 6-8)

Semi-evergreen shrub with mid-green leaves and bright yellow flowers in early spring before the new leaves appear. Height 12 in (30 cm), spread 3 ft (1 m).

Fuchsia procumbens (zones 9-10)

Prostrate deciduous shrub with mid-green heart-shaped leaves and upward-pointing

green-yellow flowers with purple-tipped green sepals in summer. These are followed by bright red fruit that look like small plums. Unfortunately this unusual fuchsia, with a height of 6 in (15 cm) and spread of 4 ft (1.2 m) is hardy only in mild, sheltered areas. If you are not lucky enough to live in such a place, try 'Golden News', hardy in all but the coldest locations and with striking pink and magenta flowers.

Gaultheria

A very useful group of evergreens.

Gaultheria cuneata (zones 4-7) is a dwarf shrub with mid-green leaves and racemes of white flowers in late spring and early summer, followed by white fruit in autumn. Height 12 in (30 cm), spread 36 in (90 cm).

Gaultheria miqueliana (zones 6-8) is compact with dark green leaves. Racemes of bell-shaped, white flowers in late spring and early summer are followed by white or pink-flushed white fruit in autumn. Height 24 in (30 cm), spread 4 ft (1.2 m).

Gaultheria myrsinoides (zones 7-8) creeps along the ground, spreading by suckers. It has dark green leaves and white flowers in early summer, followed by dark purple fruit. Height 8 in (20 cm), spread 18 in (45 cm).

Gaultheria procumbens (wintergreen) (zones 3-7) spreads in the same way and has glossy, dark green leaves that, when crushed, smell of wintergreen. The white or pale pink, urn-shaped flowers appear in summer and are followed by aromatic deep red fruit. Height 6 in (15 cm), spread 36 in (90 cm).

Gaultheria pyroloides (zones 4-8) is also flat-growing and spreads by suckers. It has dark green leaves and racemes of pink-white flowers in late spring, followed by blue-black fruit. Height 6 in (15 cm), spread 24 in (60 cm).

Gaultheria trichophylla (zones 6-9) spreads by suckers to form carpets of dark green leaves. Bell-shaped white or pink flowers in late spring are followed by pale blue fruit. Height 6 in (15 cm), spread 12 in (30 cm).

Gaultheria x *wisleyensis* 'Pink Pixie' (zones 7-9) is a vigorous spreading shrub with dark green leaves and white flowers tinged pink,

x *Halimiocistus sahucii*

followed by deep red fruit. Height 12 in (30 cm), spread 18 in (45 cm).

Genista

The brooms are a large group of deciduous shrubs, some of which make good ground cover.

Genista lydia (zones 6-9) has blue-green leaves and racemes of yellow flowers in early summer. Height 24 in (60 cm), spread 36 in (90 cm).

Genista pilosa (zones 6-9) is prostrate with dark green leaves and racemes of bright yellow flowers in late spring and early summer. Height 18 in (45 cm), spread 36 in (90 cm). *G. p.* 'Procumbens' grows to 8 in (20 cm) with yellow flowers in early summer.

Genista sagittalis (zones 5-8) is low-growing with pale green leaves and masses of deep yellow flowers in early summer. Height 6 in (15 cm), spread 36 in (90 cm).

x Halimiocistus

x *Halimiocistus* 'Ingwersenii' (zones 8-9) is a spreading evergreen with dark green leaves and saucer-shaped white flowers during spring and summer. Height 18 in (45 cm), spread 36 in (90 cm).

x *Halimiocistus sahucii* (zones 8-9) is compact, with dark green leaves and white flowers with yellow centers in summer. Height 24 in (60 cm), spread 36 in (90 cm).

x *Halimiocistus wintorensis* 'Merrist Wood Cream' (zones 7-9) is another spreader, with gray-green leaves and saucer-shaped, pale yellow flowers with a broad deep red band and yellow center in late spring and early summer. Height 24 in (60 cm), spread 36 in (90 cm).

Halimium (zones 9-10)

Halimium ocymoides is a bushy evergreen with gray-green leaves covered in white down, and terminal panicles of golden yellow flowers with deep purple centers in early summer. Height 24 in (60 cm), spread 36 in (90 cm).

Halimium 'Susan' is a spreading evergreen with gray-green leaves and bright yellow semi-double flowers with a maroon center. Height 18 in (45 cm), spread 24 in (60 cm).

Hebe

These hebes are evergreen shrubs, mostly hardy and excellent for ground cover.

Hebe albicans (zones 9-10) is a mound-former with gray-green leaves and short terminal racemes of white flowers in summer. Height 24 in (60 cm), spread 24 in (90 cm).

Hebe 'Autumn Glory' (zones 9-10) is a spreader with dark green, red-margined leaves and purple young shoots. The flowers are dark blue with white tubes from summer to winter. Height 24 in (60 cm), spread 36 in (90 cm).

Hebe 'Bowles' Variety' (zones 9-10) is compact with glossy mid-green leaves and terminal racemes of deep mauve blue flowers in summer. Height 18 in (45 cm), spread 24 in (60 cm).

Hebe buchananii (zones 8-10) is a spreader with dark green leaves and masses of white flowers in summer. Height 10 in (25 cm), spread 36 in (90 cm).

Hebe canterburiensis (zones 9-10) also spreads. It has dark green leaves and white flowers in summer. Height 24 in (60 cm), spread 36 in (90 cm). *H. c.* 'Prostrata' is lower growing with a height of 12 in (30 cm).

Hebe chathamica (zones 9-10) is a superb prostrate, ground-covering shrub that needs a warm, frost- and wind-free site. It has fleshy, shiny, deep green leaves and racemes of white flowers in early summer. Height 6 in (15 cm), spread 36 in (90 cm).

Hebe cupressoides 'Boughton Dome' (zones 8-9) is rounded, with tiny, pale green leaves along the stems. I have never seen it flower. Height 12 in (30 cm), spread 24 in (60 cm).

Hebe albicans 'Red Edge'

Hebe epacridea (zones 8-9) is low-growing with mid-green leaves and fragrant white flowers in late spring. Height 18 in (45 cm) spread 24 in (60 cm).

Hebe ochracea 'James Stirling' (zones 8-10) is a bushy whipcord shrub with deep old-gold yellow leaves and masses of white flowers in late spring and early summer. Height 18 in (45 cm), spread 36 in (90 cm).

Hebe pinguifolia 'Pagei' (zones 8-10) is semi-prostrate with leathery, blue-green leaves and purple stems. The flowers are white in late spring and early summer. Height 12 in (30 cm), spread 36 in (90 cm).

Hebe 'Red Edge' (zones 9-10) is low-growing, with gray-green, red margined leaves and terminal spikes of mid-blue flowers in summer. Height 18 in (45 cm), spread 24 in (60 cm).

Hebe 'Youngii' (zones 8-9) forms carpets of dark green leaves and produces deep blue flowers with a white throat in summer. Height 10 in (25 cm), spread 32 in (80 cm).

Hydrangea macrophylla 'Pia' (zones 6-9) Hortensia is a bushy deciduous shrub with glossy dark green leaves and bright red flowers with white centers. Height 24 in (60 cm), spread 36 in (90 cm).

Hypericum
Another useful genus of evergreens. *Hypericum balearicum* (zones 6-9) is a dumpy shrub with

Jovellana violacea

Iberis saxatilis

leathery, dark green leaves and bright yellow flowers. Height 10 in (25 cm), spread 16 in (40 cm).

Hypericum calycinum (rose of Sharon) (zones 5-9) is low-growing, spreading by runners, with shiny, dark green leaves paler on the underside and large, saucer-shaped yellow flowers in summer and early autumn. Height 24 in (60 cm), spread indefinite.

Hypericum empetrifolium (zones 4-7) forms cushions of mid-green leaves and produces masses of golden yellow flowers in summer. It will not survive very cold seasons. Height 18 in (45 cm), spread 36 in (90 cm).

Hypericum x *moserianum* 'Tricolor' (zones 7-9) is a spreader with mid-green leaves variegated with cream and pink. Cup-shaped yellow flowers are borne in summer and autumn. Requires a warm, frost- and wind-free position. Height 12 in (30 cm), spread 32 in (80 cm).

Iberis
Iberis saxatilis (zones 6-9) is an evergreen sub-shrub with thick, dark green leaves and small white flowers in late spring and early summer. Height 8 in (20 cm), spread 12 in (30 cm). For *I. sempervirens* (zones 5-9) see under **Alpines**, page 116.

Indigofera decora (zones 7-9)
Spreading, deciduous shrub with dark green leaves and racemes of white flowers flushed pink in late summer. Height 20 in (50 cm), spread 36 in (90 cm).

Jasminum parkeri (zones 7-10)
Rounded evergreen with dark green pointed leaves and bright yellow flowers in early summer followed by yellowish-white berries. Height and spread 18 in (45 cm).

Jovellana violacea (zones 9-10)
Evergreen sub-shrub that travels by suckers with deep green leaves and panicles of pale purple flowers, purple-spotted with yellow throats in summer. Height 24 in (60 cm), spread 4 ft (1.2 m).

Kalmia
Kalmia angustifolia (sheep laurel) (zones 1-6) is an evergreen with dark green leaves and cup-shaped, white, pink or red flowers in late spring and early summer. Height 2 in (60 cm), spread 5 ft (1.5 m).

Kalmia polifolia (eastern bog laurel) (zones 2-6) has racemes of saucer-shaped deep pink flowers in late spring. Height 2 in (60 cm), spread 32 in (80 cm).

Kalmiopsis leachiana 'Umpqua Valley'
(zones 7-9)
Dwarf evergreen with shiny, deep green leaves and racemes of cup-shaped, pink-purple flowers in spring. Height 12 in (30 cm), spread 18 in (45 cm).

Lavandula
For *Lavandula angustifolia*, *L. dentata* and *L. stoechas*, see under **Herbs**, page 106.
  Lavandula x *intermedia* (English lavender) (zones 5-8) is an evergreen with curved, gray-green, aromatic leaves covered in silver hairs. The flowers are pale blue appearing in long spikes in summer. Height and spread 18 in (45 cm).
  Lavandula viridis (zones 9-10) is a bushy evergreen with pale green leaves and dense spikes of white flowers above green bracts in mid- to late summer. Height 24 in (60 cm), spread 32 in (80 cm).

x Ledodendron (zones 8-10)
Hybrid genus formed as a cross between *Rhododendron trichostomum* and *Ledum grandulosum*. x *L.* 'Arctic Tern' is an evergreen shrub with hairy, dark green leaves and tubular white flowers in late spring and early summer. Height and spread 24 in (60 cm).

Ledum decumbens (zones 2-6)
Carpet-forming evergreen with aromatic mid-green leaves and pure white flowers in early summer. Height 10 in (25 cm), spread 36 in (90 cm).

Leiophyllum buxifolium (zones 6-8)
Suckering evergreen with shiny, dark green leaves that turn bronze in winter and white flowers opening from pink buds in late spring and early summer. Height 18 in (45 cm), spread 24 in (60 cm).

Leptospermum 'Rupestre' (zones 9-10)
Prostrate evergreen with tiny, deep green, aromatic leaves and small white flowers in late spring and summer. Height 18 in (45 cm), spread 4 ft (1.2 m).

Linnaea borealis (zones 2-6)
Carpet-forming evergreen with shiny, deep green leaves pale green on the underside and pale pink bell-shaped flowers on short stalks from the ends of the side shoots during summer. Height 4 in (10 cm), spread 36 in (90 cm). *L. b.* 'Americana' has longer, pale green leaves with white flowers in late spring. Height 4 in (10 cm), spread 12 in (30 cm).

Linum arboreum (zones 6-9)
Dwarf evergreen with leathery dark green leaves and deep yellow flowers in late spring and summer. It requires a sheltered site. Height and spread 18 in (45 cm).

Lithodora
For *Lithodora diffusa* 'Heavenly Blue', see under **Alpines**, page 116.
  Lithodora rosmarinifolia (zones 8-10) is an evergreen sub-shrub with dark green leaves and bright blue flowers in summer. Height 12 in (30 cm), spread 18 in (45 cm). The leaves of *L. zahnii* are also dark green but gray on the underside. Mid-blue or white flowers appear in summer and autumn. It is not completely hardy. Height and spread 18 in (45 cm).

Loiseleuria procumbens (zones 2-5)
Alpine azalea is an evergreen, prostrate shrub with shiny, dark green leaves and cup-shaped pink or white flowers in late spring and early summer. Height 4 in (10 cm), spread 12 in (30 cm).

Lonicera pileata (zones 5-9)
Dense, spreading evergreen, ideal for ground cover, with shiny, dark green leaves and small creamy-white flowers in late spring, followed by purple berries. Height 24 in (60 cm), spread 10 ft (3 m).

Mahonia (zones 6-9)
All the species given here are suckering evergreen shrubs. *Mahonia aquifolium* 'Atropurpurea' has shiny green, spiny-toothed leaves that turn plum red in autumn and racemes of bright yellow flowers in spring followed by blue-black berries. Height 24 in (60 cm), spread 36 in (90 cm). The variety *M. a.* 'Orange Flame' has a similar height and spreads and produces orange-colored young foliage that turns red in autumn.

Mahonia nervosa (zones 6-8) has shiny, dark green leaves that turn purple in winter and racemes of pale yellow flowers in late spring, followed by blue-black berries. Height 18 in (45 cm), spread 4 ft (1.2 m). *M. pumila* is low-growing, with gray-green, spiny leaves and dark yellow flowers in spring followed by blue black berries. Height 12 in (30 cm), spread 36 in (90 cm). The dull green leaves of *M. repens* have wavy margins. Dark yellow flowers in late spring are followed by blue-black berries. Height 10 in (25 cm), spread 36 in (90 cm).

Linum arboreum

Moltkia x intermedia (zones 7-9)
Evergreen sub-shrub with dark green leaves and funnel-shaped, bright blue flowers in early summer. Height and spread 12 in (30 cm).

Myrteola nummularia (zones 9-10)
Carpet-forming evergreen sub-shrub with tiny, dark green leaves and small white flowers in early summer, followed by pink berries. Height 2 in (5 cm), 12 in spread (30 cm).

Ozothamnus
Ozothamnus coralloides (zones 8-9) is a compact evergreen with tiny, leathery, green leaves gray on the underside and flattened to the stem. Pale yellow flowers appear in summer. Height and spread 28 in (70 cm). *O. selago* (zones 9-10) is also evergreen, with tiny, pale green, aromatic leaves and cream flowers in summer. Height 18 in (45 cm), 12 in spread (30 cm).

Parahebe

Another group of useful evergreens, broadly similar to the hebes. *Parahebe* x *bidwillii* 'Kea' (zones 9-10) is a carpet-forming sub-shrub with thick, dark green leaves and white flowers with deep red veins in summer. Height and spread 6 in (15 cm).

Parahebe catarractaea (zones 9-10) is an evergreen shrub with dark green leaves and white flowers with purple veins and red centers in summer. Height 12 in (30 cm), spread 18 in (45 cm).

Parahebe hookeriana (zones 8-10) is a carpet-forming sub-shrub with leathery, mid-green leaves and racemes of lavender or pale blue flowers with a red center in summer. Height 8 in (20 cm), spread 24 in (60 cm).

Parahebe lyallii (zones 8-9) is a prostrate evergreen shrub with leathery, dark green leaves and saucer-shaped, white or pink flowers with purple veins and red centers in early summer. Height 12 in (30 cm), spread 24 in (60 cm).

Paxistima canbyi (zones 3-7)

Spreading evergreen with glossy, deep green leaves and clusters of green-white flowers in summer. Height 18 in (45 cm), spread 36 in (90 cm).

Penstemon

A genus of useful evergreen sub-shrubs.

Prostanthera cuneata

Penstemon cardwellii (zones 6-9) is a spreader with mid-green leaves and panicles of deep purple, funnel-shaped flowers in early summer. Height 8 in (20 cm), spread 12 in (30 cm). *P. davidsonii* (zones 5-9) is prostrate with leathery, pale green leaves and panicles of deep pink flowers in late spring and early summer. Height 12 in (30 cm), spread 18 in (45 cm). *P. fruticosus* (shrubby penstemon) (zones 4-9) has shiny, mid-green leaves and racemes of deep red-blue flowers in late spring and early summer. Height and spread 18 in (45 cm).

Petrophytum (zones 6-9)

Petrophytum caespitosum is a flat-growing evergreen sub-shrub with blue-green leaves and tiny, creamy white flowers with long stamens in summer. Height 2 in (5 cm), spread 12 in (30 cm). *P. hendersonii* is a rounded evergreen sub-shrub with blue-green leaves and racemes of creamy white flowers in summer. Height 4 in (10 cm) spread 12 in (30 cm).

Phlomis

Phlomis italica (zones 9-10) is evergreen with woolly leaves and mauve-pink flowers in summer. Height 12 in (30 cm), spread 24 in (60 cm). *P. purpurea* (zones 9-10) has gray-green leaves woolly on the underside and purple, sometimes white flowers in summer. *P. purpurea* requires a sheltered site. Height and spread 28 in (70 cm).

Phyllodoce

Another useful group of evergreens. *Phyllodoce aleutica* (zones 2-5) is carpet-forming with shiny, dark green leaves, pale green with a central white line on the underside, and urn-shaped green-yellow flowers in late spring and early summer. Height and spread 12 in (30 cm). *P. caerulea* (zones 2-5) has shiny, dark green leaves and clusters of deep pink flowers in late spring and summer. Height 8 in (20 cm), spread 12 in (30 cm). *P empetriformis* (zones 3-6) also forms a carpet. It has bright, dark green leaves and clusters of rosy pink, bell-shaped flowers in spring and early summer. Height and spread 12 in (30 cm)

Pieris

Pieris japonica 'Little Heath' (zones 6-8) is a compact, rounded evergreen with mid-green leaves that are quite pink when young and edged silvery white. Terminal panicles of white flowers appear in early spring. Height and spread 24 in (60 cm). The dwarf *P. nana* (zones 3-6) is a cushion-forming evergreen shrub with leathery, dark green leaves tinted red in winter and early spring and terminal panicles of white flowers in late spring and early summer. Height 4 in (10 cm), spread 12 in (30 cm).

Pimelea prostrata (zones 9-10)

Compact, spreading evergreen with tiny, gray-green, leathery leaves that are edged red and fragrant white flowers in summer, followed by small white or red fruit. Requires a sheltered, frost-free site. Height 8 in (20 cm), spread 24 in (60 cm).

Potentilla fruticosa (zones 3-7)

A species of deciduous bushy shrubs with a number of useful varieties. *P. f.* 'Beesii' has silky silver leaves and golden yellow flowers all summer. Height 24 in (60 cm), spread 4 ft (1.2 m). 'Manchu' is a dwarf form with silvery gray leaves on red shoots and white flowers from late spring until early autumn. Height 12 in (30 cm), spread 36 in (90 cm). The low-growing variety 'Princess' has mid-green leaves and pale pink flowers all summer. Height 24 in (60 cm), spread 36 in (90 cm). 'Tilford Cream' is low and spreading with pale green leaves and cream flowers from late spring until late summer. Height 24 in (60 cm), spread 36 in (90 cm).

Prostanthera cuneata (zones 9-10)

Mint bush is a spreading evergreen with shiny, dark green leaves that are aromatic (smelling of mint) when crushed. Racemes of white flowers with yellow and purple markings appear in summer. Height 24 in (60 cm), spread 4 ft (1.2 m).

Putoria calabrica (zones 8-9)

Stinking madder is an evergreen spreading shrub with leathery mid-green leaves that have an absolutely awful smell when crushed, but makes a good ground-cover plant if you have dry, sandy soil in full sun. The best advice that I can give is not to plant it where it might be walked on. The terminal clusters of pink flowers are produced all summer. Height 4 in (10 cm), spread 12 in (30 cm).

Rhododendron
All the varieties of this vast genus recommended here are evergreen; the following are dwarfs. *Rhododendron* 'Blue Tit' (zones 7-9) is compact-growing with mid-green leaves that are pale green when they first appear. Funnel-shaped pale blue flowers appear in early spring. Height and spread 36 in (90 cm). *R. calostotum* (zones 7-9) has blue-green leaves with brown scales on the underside and saucer-shaped, deep pink flowers with purple spots on the upper lobes in late spring and early summer. Height 24 in (60 cm), spread 36 in (90 cm). The leaves of *R.* 'Chikor' (zones 7-9) are dark green, turning bronze in winter. Bright yellow flowers appear in spring. Height and spread 24 in (60 cm). *R.* 'Ginny Gee' (zones 6-9) is a dense shrub with small, dark green leaves and mauve-pink flowers in mid-spring. Height 24 in (60 cm), spread 36 in (90 cm).

Rhododendron 'Hino-crimson' (zones 5-8) and *R.* 'Hino-mayo' are both dwarf evergreen members of the Japanese group *Kurume* azaleas with a height and spread of 24 in (60 cm). *R.* 'Hino-crimson' has mid-green leaves and masses of brilliant red flowers in spring. *R.* 'Hino-mayo' (zones 7-9) has shiny, dark green leaves and masses of funnel-shaped bright pink flowers in late spring and early summer.

Rhododendron impeditum (zones 5-8) is another dwarf with small, gray-green, aromatic leaves and purplish-blue flowers in late spring. Height 24 in (60 cm), spread 36 in (90 cm).

Rhododendron 'Moerheim' (zones 6-9) is a small shrub with dark green leaves that turn deep red in winter and violet-blue flowers in late spring. Height and spread 24 in (60 cm).

Rhododendron pemakoense (zones 7-9) is compact with glossy, dark green leaves and bell-shaped, deep purple-pink flowers in mid-spring. Height 24 in (60 cm), spread 32 in (80 cm).

Rhododendron sargentianum (zones 7-9) has

Rosa 'Flower Carpet'

aromatic leaves which are glossy light green above with yellow scales on the underside. Creamy yellow flowers appear in late spring and early summer. Height and spread 24 in (60 cm).

Rhodothamnus chamaecistus (zones 7-9)
Prostrate evergreen with bright, dark green leaves with stiff white hairs along the edge. Pale pink flowers with red eyes appear in late spring and early summer. Height 8 in (20 cm), spread 12 in (30 cm).

Ribes alpinum (zones 2-6)
Compact deciduous shrub, related to the currant family. It has mid-green leaves and racemes of bell-shaped, greenish-yellow flowers in spring, followed by dark red fruit on female plants. Height 24 in (60 cm), spread 36 in (90 cm).

Rosa
Rosa is an enormous genus of deciduous and semi-evergreen shrubs and climbers that can be used in formal or informal landscaping. Recent introductions – including the 'County' varieties, such as 'Essex' and 'Hampshire', and those named after birds, such as 'Pheasant' and 'Grouse' – are lower-growing with long-lasting foliage and are ideal for ground covering.

Rosa 'Essex' (zones 5-9) is a dense ground-cover rose with shiny, dark green leaves and clusters of single, reddish-pink flowers with light pink centers in summer and autumn. Height 24 in (60 cm), 4 ft spread (1.2 m).

Rosa 'Flower Carpet' (zones 5-9) has a similar height and spread, shiny, bright green leaves and clusters of double rose-pink flowers in summer and autumn.

Rosa rugosa 'Fru Dagmar Hastrup' (zones 3-9) has leathery, mid-green leaves and single, pale pink, clove-scented flowers in summer, followed by large dark red, tomato-shaped hips in autumn. Height 24 in (60 cm), spread 4 ft (1.2 m).

Rosa 'Grouse' (zones 5-9) is a vigorous, trailing ground-cover rose with shiny, dark green leaves and single, pale pink, scented flowers in summer. Height 24 in (60 cm), spread 10 ft (3 m).

Rosa 'Hampshire' (zones 5-9) is a prostrate rose with shiny, mid-green leaves and single scarlet flowers with yellow centers in summer. Height 12 in (30 cm), spread 36 in (90 cm).

Rosa 'Hertfordshire' (zones 5-9) is a compact rose with bright dark green leaves and clusters of single, deep pink flowers with pale pink centers in summer and autumn. Height 18 in (45 cm), spread 36 in (90 cm).

The vigorous, trailing *Rosa* 'Nozomi' (zones 5-9) has shiny, dark green leaves and masses of clusters of single, white-flushed pale pink flowers in summer. Height 18 in (45 cm), spread 6 ft 6 in (2 m).

Rosa 'Pheasant' (zones 5-9) is a creeping ground-coverer with shiny, dark green leaves and clusters of double pink flowers with yellow stamens in summer. Height 20 in (50 cm), spread 10 ft (3 m).

Rosa pimpinellifolia (Scots' rose or burnet rose) (zones 3-9) is prickly and spreads by suckers. It has dark green, fern-like leaves and creamy white flowers in early summer, followed by purple-black hips. Height 24 in (60 cm), spread 36 in (90 cm).

Rosa 'Red Blanket' (zones 5-9) is a spreading ground-coverer with dark green leaves and clusters of semi-double, rose-red flowers in summer and autumn. Height 24 in (60 cm), spread 5 ft (1.5 m).

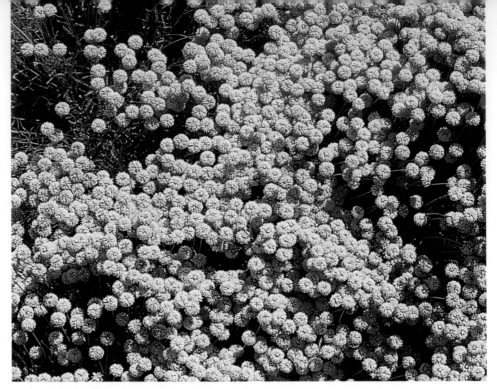

Santolina chamaecyparissus 'Lemon Queen'

The dense dwarf variety *Rosa* 'Robin Redbreast' (zones 5-9) has shiny, light green leaves and clusters of single, dark red flowers with white centers in summer and autumn. Height 18 in (45 cm), spread 30 in (75 cm).

Rosa 'Surrey' (zones 5-9) is a vigorous shrub rose with dark green leaves and clusters of double, pink flowers in summer and autumn. Height 24 in (60 cm), spread 5 ft (1.5 m). *Rosa* 'Swany' (zones 5-9) has shiny, dark green leaves and clusters of double white flowers in summer and autumn. Height 24 in (60 cm), spread 6 ft 6 in (2 m).

Rosmarinus
See under **Herbs**, page 107.

Rubus (zones 7-9)
Rubus species that are grown for their berries are included under **Fruit** (see page 111), but many others are highly ornamental, low-growing evergreens spreading quickly to form good ground cover.

Rubus 'Betty Ashburner' is a prostrate evergreen with glossy, mid-green leaves, shoots covered in red bristles, and saucer-shaped white flowers at the leaf axils. Height 12 in (30 cm), spread indefinite. *Rubus pentalobus* is more

vigorous. Its dark green leaves have wrinkled edges and its white flowers appear in summer. Height 4 in (10 cm), spread indefinite. The equally vigorous *R. tricolor* has glossy, dark green leaves, hairy-white underneath and shoots covered in red bristles. Racemes of white flowers in summer are followed by raspberry-like, edible, deep red fruit in autumn. Height 24 in (60 cm), spread indefinite.

Ruscus
Ruscus hypoglossum (zones 7-9) is an evergreen, sucker-spreading sub-shrub spreading with shiny green cladophylls that resemble leaves but are really flattened stems. Female plants produce red berries on the cladophylls in autumn and winter. Height 18 in (45 cm), spread 4 ft (1.2 m). *R. hypophyllum* (zones 8-10) spreads by rhizomes, with pointed, dark green clado-phylls and red berries produced by female plants on the cladophylls during late summer and winter. Height 24 in (60 cm), spread 36 in (90 cm).

Salix
The willows are all deciduous, producing their spring flowers as catkins either before

or at the same time as the leaves. *Salix apoda* (zones 5-8) is a prostrate with leathery, dark green leaves and silvery male catkins that turn orange as they age, appearing in early spring. Height 10 in (25 cm), spread 36 in (90 cm).

Salix helvetica (Swiss willow) (zones 5-8) is upright with gray-green leaves silvery on the underside and golden buds opening to silver catkins in late winter. The prostrate *S. repens* (creeping willow) (zones 5-7) has similar leaves. Its gray catkins have deep yellow anthers and open in late spring. Both grow to a height of 24 in (60 cm) with a spread of 6 ft (1. 8 m).

Salix retusa and *S. serpyllifolia* (thyme-leafed willow) are both carpeting shrubs. *S. retusa* has shiny mid-green leaves and gray catkins in spring as the leaves appear. Height 4 in (10 cm), spread 20 in (50 cm). *S. serpyllifolia* has mid-green leaves and silvery catkins in spring. Height 1 in (3 cm), spread 18 in (45 cm).

Santolina chamaecyparissus (zones 6-9)

Cotton lavender is a compact evergreen with aromatic, gray-green leaves, white woolly shoots and then yellow flowerheads in late summer. Height 24 in (60 cm), spread 36 in (90 cm). The variety *S. c.* 'Lemon Queen' has pale yellow flowers with a height and spread of 24 in (60 cm).

Sarcococca humilis (zones 6-9)

Christmas box or sweet box is a dwarf, evergreen, suckering shrub with shiny, dark green leaves and clusters of fragrant white flowers flushed pink in winter, followed by blue-black fruit. Height 24 in (60 cm), spread 4 ft (1.2 m).

Satureja spicigera (zones 7-8)

Creeping, aromatic sub-shrub with mid-green leaves and white flowers in summer. Height 6 in (15 cm), spread 18 in (45 cm).

Senecio

Senecio abrotanifolius (zones 6-9) is an evergreen shrub with glossy, deep green leaves and deep orange-yellow flowers in

summer and early autumn. Height and spread 12 in (30 cm).

Senecio cineraria (zones 8-10) requires a warm, wind- and frost-free site and is usually grown as an annual. It has felted silvery gray leaves and if grown as a shrub has deep yellow flowers in the summer of the second year. Height and spread 32 in (80 cm).

Skimmia japonica 'Fructu Albo' (zones 7-9)

Compact evergreen with aromatic, dark green leaves and panicles of scented flowers opening from green buds in late spring, followed by white fruits. Height 20 in (50 cm), spread 36 in (90 cm).

Spiraea japonica (zones 4-9)

This is just one of about 80 species of spiraea. It is one of the best for summer show, holding its flowers above the dense cover of deciduous leaves.

Spiraea japonica 'Allgold' is a deciduous, clump-forming shrub with golden yellow leaves and pink flowers in mid-and late summer. Height 18 in (45 cm), spread 24 in (60 cm). *S. j.* 'Bullata'. is compact and slow-growing, with dark green leaves and dark pink flowers in summer. Height and spread 20 in (50 cm).

The variety *Spiraea japonica* 'Little Princess' forms a dense mound, with small mid-green leaves and rose-pink flowers in summer and early autumn. Height 18 in (45 cm), spread 36 in (90 cm). 'Shirobana' also forms a mound, with mid-green leaves. The flowers are unusual in that white and pink blooms appear on the same stem. Height and spread 24 in (60 cm).

Stachys candida (zones 5-8)

Spreading evergreen sub-shrub with white-felted, gray-green leaves and spikes of white flowers with purple spots in summer. Height 8 in (20 cm), spread 12 in (30 cm).

Stephanandra incisa 'Crispa' (zones 5-8)

Deciduous shrub spreading by suckers, with mid-green, wavy-edged leaves that turn brilliant orange-yellow in autumn and panicles of greenish-white flowers in early summer. Height and spread 24 in (60 cm).

Teucrium fruticans (zones 8-9)

Shrubby germander is a bushy evergreen with aromatic, gray-green leaves, woolly-white underneath, and racemes of pale blue flowers in summer. It requires a sheltered site. Height 24 in (60 cm), spread 13 ft (4 m).

Tsusiophyllum tanakae (zones 6-9)

Prostrate evergreen with hairy dark green leaves and clusters of silky white flowers produced at the tips of the shoots in early summer. It does best in partial shade such as woodland. Height 18 in (45 cm), spread 12 in (30 cm).

Vaccinium

This is a versatile group of plants that includes cranberry and the blueberries, grown for their edible berries and described under **Fruit** (see page 111). All the *Vaccinium* enjoy acid, peaty soil in woodland conditions.

Vaccinium caespitosum (dwarf bilberry) (zones 2-7) is a vigorous, spreading, deciduous shrub with dark green leaves and white or pink, urn-shaped flowers in late spring and early summer, followed by blue-black berries. Height 6 in (15 cm), spread 24 in (60 cm).

Vaccinium crassifolium (creeping blueberry) (zones 6-8) is a vigorous, carpeting evergreen with thick, leathery, dark green leaves and racemes of white or deep pink, urn-shaped flowers, followed by deep purple fruit. Height 18 in (45 cm), spread 4 ft (1.2 m).

Vaccinium delavayi (zones 7-9) is a spreading evergreen with leathery, dark green leaves and creamy white flowers in early summer, followed by deep red berries. Height 24 in (60 cm), spread 4 ft (1.2 m).

Vaccinium myrtillus (bilberry or whortleberry) (zones 5-7) is a vigorous, creeping, deciduous shrub with shiny, bright green leaves and urn-shaped pink flowers in late spring and early summer, followed by blue-black berries. Height 12 in (30 cm), spread indefinite and likely to become invasive.

Vinca

The periwinkles are trailing evergreens, useful in shade but better in sun if you want lots of flowers.

Vinca difformis (periwinkle) (zones 8-9) is a prostrate sub-shrub with shiny, dark green leaves and white-with-a-hint-of-pale-blue flowers in winter and early spring. Slightly tender. Height 12 in (30 cm), spread indefinite.

Vinca major (greater periwinkle) (zones 7-11) is vigorous, with dark green leaves and dark violet flowers from late spring until autumn. Height 18 in (45 cm), spread indefinite. The leaves of the variety *V. m.* 'Variegata' are edged creamy white, and those of *V. m.* 'Maculata' have pale yellow centers.

Vinca minor (lesser periwinkle) (zones 4-9) is a prostrate, carpet-forming shrub with dark green leaves and white, pale blue, purple or violet flowers in spring, summer and autumn. Height 8 in (20 cm), spread indefinite. The variety *V. m.* 'Argenteo-variegata' has leaves with creamy white edges and violet flowers. *V. m.* 'Multiplex' has double burgundy-purple flowers.

Xanthorhiza simplicissima (zones 3-9)

Deciduous shrub with long, bright green leaves that turn red in autumn and brown-purple flowers in spring. Height 24 in (60 cm), spread 6 ft (1.8 m).

Yucca flaccida (zones 5-9)

Clump-forming evergreen with a rosette of lance-like, dark blue-green leaves edged with curled cream threads and tall panicles of bell-shaped, white flowers in summer. Height 24 in (60 cm), spread 5 ft (1.5 m). The variety *Y. f.* 'Golden Sword' has yellow-edged leaves.

MEDIUM-GROWING

Abelia x grandiflora 'Francis Mason' (zones 6-9)
Rounded, evergreen shrub with bright yellow leaves marked dark green and terminal panicles of fragrant white flowers, tinged pink, in late summer and early autumn. Height and spread 6 ft (1.8 m).

Aesculus parviflora (zones 5-9)
Suckering deciduous shrub with typically chestnut-shaped leaves appearing bronze and turning to mid-green and conical panicles of white flowers in early summer, followed by smooth-skinned fruit. Height 10 ft (3 m), spread 16 ft (5 m).

Arctostaphylos patula (zones 6-9)
Spreading, evergreen with leathery, bright green leaves and panicles of white or pink flowers in late spring and early summer, followed by black fruit in early autumn. Height and spread 6 ft (1.8 m).

Artemisia
Artemisia abrotanum (southernwood, lad's love) (zones 5-8) is a semi-evergreen shrub with aromatic, gray-green leaves and panicles of yellowish-green flowers in late summer. Height and spread 36 in (90 cm). *A. arborescens* (zones 5-9) is evergreen, with aromatic silver leaves and panicles of yellow flowers in summer and early autumn. Height 36 in (90 cm), spread 6 ft (1.8 m).

Aucuba japonica (zones 6-10)
Aucuba japonica 'Crotonifolia' is an evergreen with glossy, mid-green leaves speckled bright yellow and purple flowers in spring, followed by bright red berries. Height and spread 10 ft (3 m). The more compact *A. j.* 'Rozannie' has glossy, dark green leaves and bisexual flowers, followed by large bright red fruit. Height and spread 4 ft (1.2 m).

Berberis
With their spiny leaves and sharp thorns, berberis are not only good deterrent plants, but the evergreen varieties make excellent ground cover with a dense canopy of leaves.

Xanthorhiza simplicissima

Artemisia arborescens

Berberis x *bristolensis* (zones 6-9) is a mound-forming, evergreen with shiny, dark green, spiny leaves glaucous on the underside and turning red in autumn. Yellow flowers in spring are followed by blue-black fruit. Height and spread 6 ft (1. 8 m). The more compact *B. calliantha* (zones 7-9) has spiny, dark green leaves waxy white on the underside and pale yellow flowers in late spring, followed by black fruit. Height and spread 36 in (90 cm).

Berberis chenaultii (zones 6-9) is a spreader, with dark green, spiny leaves glaucous on the underside and turning bronze in winter. Bright yellow flowers in spring are followed by blue-black fruit. Height and spread 5 ft (1.5 m).

Berberis x *frikartii* 'Telstar' (zones 6-9) is compact with shiny, dark green leaves white on the underside and clusters of yellow

Betula nana

flowers in late spring, followed by blue-black fruit. Height and spread 4 ft (1.2 m).

The mound-forming *Berberis* x *interposita* 'Wallich's Purple' (zones 7-9) has spiny, bronze leaves, turning mid-green. Yellow flowers appear in spring and are followed by blue-black fruit. Height 4 ft (1.2 m), spread 6 ft (1.8 m).

Betula nana (zones 2-5)
Arctic birch is a rounded, deciduous shrub with shiny, light green leaves that turn red and yellow in autumn and deep orange-yellow, male catkins in spring. Height 24 in (60 cm), spread 4 ft (1.2 m).

Brachyglottis
Brachyglottis compacta (zones 8-9) is a compact, evergreen shrub with dark green leaves, white-hairy when young, and bright yellow flowers in summer. Height 36 in (90 cm), spread 6 ft (1.8 m). *B.* 'Dunedin Hybrids' (zones 9-10) is a spreading variety, with dark green leaves, white-hairy when young, and bright yellow daisy-like flowers in summer and autumn. Height 5 ft (1.5 m), spread 10 ft (3 m).

Buddleia officinalis (zones 9-10)
Upright evergreen with dark green leaves gray on the underside and fragrant panicles of violet flowers with yellow eyes in winter and early spring. Height and spread 8 ft (2.5 m).

Bupleurum fruticosum (zones 7-10)
Sometimes known as shrubby hare's ear, this is a dense evergreen shrub with blue-green leaves and star-shaped, yellow flowers in summer and early autumn. Height and spread 6 ft (1.8 m).

Buxus
Buxus microphylla (small-leafed box) (zones 6-9) is a dense, evergreen, slow-growing shrub with dark green leaves turning bronze in winter and tiny yellow-green flowers in spring. Height 32 in (80 cm), spread 4 ft (1.2 m). *B. sempervirens* 'Suffruticosa' (zones 6-8) is a bushy, compact, evergreen with glossy, dark green leaves and insignificant flowers. Very slow-growing and ideal as a dwarf hedge. Height 36 in (90 cm), spread 4 ft (1.2 m).

Callistemon
Callistemon citrinus 'Austraflora Firebrand' (bottlebrush) (zones 10-11) is a spreading evergreen with dark green leaves, silver-pink new growths and bright crimson spikes of flowers in early summer. Height 6 ft (1.8 m), spread 13 ft (4 m). *C. pityoides* (alpine bottlebrush) (zones 9-10) is more compact, with dark green, pointed leaves and yellow spikes of flowers in summer. Height 5 ft (1.5 m), spread 36 in (90 cm).

Callistemon citrinus

Calycanthus floridus (zones 5-9)
Carolina allspice, also sometimes known as strawberry bush, is a spreading, deciduous shrub with dark green leaves and deep red flowers in summer. Height and spread 10 ft (3 m).

Carpenteria californica (zones 8-9)
Bushy evergreen shrubs with glossy, dark green leaves and peeling, orange-brown bark. The cup-shaped, fragrant, white flowers with bright yellow stamens appear in midsummer. Height and spread 6 ft (1. 8 m).

Ceanothus

A useful genus of spreading evergreen shrubs, one of the few plants to produce genuinely blue flowers.

Ceanothus 'A. T. Johnson' (zones 9-10) is vigorous, with pale green leaves and terminal panicles of deep blue flowers in spring, repeating in late summer and autumn. Height and spread 8 ft (2.5 m). *C. divergens* (zones 8-10) is lower growing, with dark green leaves and deep blue flowers in spring. Height 36 in (90 cm), spread 4 ft (1.2 m).

Ceanothus 'Italian Skies' (zones 9-10) has glossy, light green leaves and bright blue flowers in spring. Height 4 ft (1.2 m), spread 10 ft (3 m). The compact *C.* 'Southmead' (zones 9-10) has finely toothed, dark green leaves and dark blue flowers in spring and early summer. Height and spread 4 ft (1.2 m).

Ceratostigma willmottianum (zones 6-9)

Spreading deciduous shrub with bristly, dark green leaves with purple edges turning red in autumn and clusters of pale blue flowers in late summer and autumn. Height 36 in (90 cm), spread 6 ft (1.8 m).

Chaenomeles x superba (zones 5-9)

Rounded, spiny, deciduous shrub with shiny, mid-green leaves and white, pink, orange or crimson cup-shaped flowers in spring, often before the leaves, followed by hard green fruit that turn golden yellow. Height 4 ft (1.2 m), spread 6 ft (1.8 m).

The variety *Chaenomeles* x *superba* 'Crimson and Gold' has a more spreading habit, shiny, mid-green leaves and dark red flowers with golden yellow anthers. Height 36 in (90 cm), spread 6 ft (1.8 m). *C.* x *s.* 'Rowallane' has dark green leaves and bright scarlet flowers that start to appear before the leaves. Height 36 in (90 cm), spread 5 ft (1.5 m).

Chamaedaphne calyculata (zones 3-9)

Leatherleaf is a low-growing evergreen with glossy, dark green, leathery leaves and urn-shaped white flowers appearing at the ends of the shoots in spring. Height and spread 32 in (80 cm).

Deutzia gracilis

Choisya (zones 7-10)

Choisya 'Aztec Pearl' is an evergreen with aromatic, dark green leaves and pink-tinged white flowers in spring and again in late summer and autumn. Height and spread 8 ft (2.5 m). *C. ternata* (Mexican orange blossom) is more compact, with shiny, aromatic, dark green leaves and fragrant white flowers in late spring and again in late summer and autumn. Height and spread 8 ft (2.5 m).

Cistus

Commonly called rock roses or sun roses, a cistus bloom resembles a large single rose with its tissue-paper-like petals. The cistuses are all evergreen and flower best in a well-drained, light soil in full sun.

Cistus x *corbariensis* (zones 8-10) is bushy, with dark green leaves. White flowers with yellow centers and stamens open from deep pink buds in late spring and summer. Height 36 in (90 cm), spread 4 ft (1.2 m). *C.* x *cyprius* (zones 8-10) has sticky dark green leaves. The white summer flowers have dark crimson and yellow blotches at the base of each petal and yellow stamens. Height and spread 4 ft (1.2 m).

Cistus x *florentinus* (zones 9-10) is more compact, with gray-green, wavy-edged leaves and white flowers with yellow centers in summer. Height 36 in (90 cm), spread 4 ft (1.2 m).

Cistus x *purpureus* (zones 9-10) is bushy with dark green leaves and sticky red shoots. The dark pink summer flowers, with crinkled petals like tissue paper, have a dark maroon blotch at the base of the petals. Height and spread 4 ft (1.2 m).

Clerodendrum bungei (zones 7-10)

Glory flower is a deciduous shrub that spreads by suckers. It has dark green leaves tinged purple when young and terminal panicles of dark pink fragrant flowers in late summer and autumn. Height and spread 10 ft (3 m).

Clethra fargesii (zones 6-8)

Deciduous shrub with dark green leaves and good yellow and red leaf color in autumn. Terminal racemes of cup-shaped white flowers appear in late summer and autumn. Height and spread 10 ft (3 m).

Cornus (zones 2-8)

This genus is probably best known for the 'dogwoods' with their brilliant winter stem coloring, which is improved if the plant is grown in full sun. Prune older stems close ot the ground in spring to encourage the new young stems that have the best color.

Cornus alba 'Elegantissima' is a vigorous deciduous shrub with red-barked shoots especially in winter and gray-green leaves margined white. Small white flowers appear in late spring and early summer, followed by white fruit. Height and spread 10 ft (3 m). *C. stolonifera* 'Flaviramea' is also vigorous, spreading by suckers, with bright yellow-green winter shoots and white flowers in spring and summer, followed by white fruit. Height 36 in (90 cm), spread 5 ft (1.5 m).

Corokia cotoneaster (zones 9-10)
Wire-netting bush is a densely branched evergreen with dark green leaves and fragrant yellow flowers in spring, followed by red or yellow fruit. Height and spread 8 ft (2.5 m).

Coronilla valentina (zones 8-9)
Bushy evergreen with bright green leaves and bright yellow flowers in winter, early spring and in summer. Height and spread 5 ft (1.5 m).

Cotoneaster
These are great garden plants, producing berries every year and tolerating most soil conditions. Lower-growing varieties are described on page 138. All those listed here are evergreen.

Cotoneaster conspicuus (zones 6-8) is mound-forming with dark green leaves and shiny red fruit in winter. Height 5 ft (1.5 m), spread 8 ft (2.5 m). *C.* 'Coral Beauty' (zones 7-8) also forms mounds, with glossy, dark green leaves and tiny white flowers in summer, followed by bright orange fruit. Height 36 in (90 cm) spread 6 ft (1.8 m).

Cotoneaster integrifolius (zones 6-8) is compact, with glossy, dark green leaves and white flowers in early summer, followed by purple-pink fruit. Height 36 in (90 cm) spread 4 ft (1.2 m). *C. linearifolius* (zones 6-8) is similar, but it has dark red fruit and spreads to only 36 in (90 cm). *C. rotundifolius* (zones 7-8) is a spreader with purple-red fruit. Height 4 ft (1.2 m), spread 10 ft (3 m).

Cytisus (zones 6-9)
The brooms are deciduous shrubs with dark leaves. All those given here reach a height and spread of 4 ft (1.2 m). *Cytisus* 'Killiney Red'

has red flowers with darker wings in late spring and early summer. *C.* 'Lena' has yellow flowers with the wings bright red and *C.* 'Zeelandii' has cream and pink flowers.

Daphne
All the daphnes listed here are evergreen with the bonus of sweetly scented flowers. More of the species are described under **Low-growing Shrubs** (page 138)

Daphne acutiloba (zones 7-9) is a spreading shrub with bright green leaves and terminal clusters of white, scented flowers in summer, followed by bright red fruit. Height and spread 5 ft (1.5 m).

Daphne laureola (spurge laurel) (zones 7-8) is bushier, with leathery, dark green leaves and fragrant, yellow-green flowers in late winter and early spring, followed by black fruit. Height 36 in (90 cm), spread 5 ft (1.5 m).

Daphne longilobata (zones 6-9) is another spreader, with glossy, mid-green leaves and terminal clusters of fragrant, white, hairy flowers in late spring and early summer, followed by shiny red fruit. Height and spread 4 ft (1.2 m).

Daphne odora (zones 7-9) has shiny, dark green leaves and fragrant purple and white flowers in winter and early spring, followed by red fruit. Height and spread 5 ft (1.5 m).

Daphne retusa (zones 7-9) is a dwarf form, with glossy, dark green leaves and terminal clusters of deep pink-red flowers, white on the inside, in spring and early summer, followed by red fruit. Height and spread 32 in (80 cm).

Desfontainia spinosa (zones 8-10)
Bushy evergreen with glossy, spiny, dark green leaves and tubular red flowers with yellow tips in summer and autumn. Height and spread 6 ft (1.8 m).

Deutzia gracilis (zones 5-8)
Deciduous with bright green leaves and racemes of fragrant, star-like, white flowers in late spring and early summer. Height and spread 4 ft (1.2 m).

Eleagnus x ebbingei 'Limelight' (zones 7-10)
Rounded evergreen with leathery, dark green leaves marked with pale green and

gold. The emerging young leaves are silvery green. Creamy white flowers are produced in autumn. Height and spread 10 ft (3 m).

Escallonia
These evergreens tolerate exposed coastal gardens and make excellent windbreaks.

Escallonia 'Edinensis' (zones 7-9) is bushy with glossy, dark green leaves and racemes of pale pink-red flowers in summer. Height 6 ft (1.8 m), spread 10 ft (3 m). *E.* 'Langleyensis' (zones 8-9) has shiny, dark green leaves and racemes of rosy-red flowers in late spring and early summer. Height 6 ft (1.8 m), spread 10 ft (3 m). *E.* 'Pride of Donard' (zones 8-9) is compact with similar leaves and short racemes of bright red flowers in early and mid-summer. Height 6ft (1.8 m), spread 10 ft (3 m).

Euonymus fortunei 'Sarcoxie' (zones 5-9)
Vigorous evergreen shrub with shiny dark green leaves and small white flowers. Height and spread 36 in (90 cm).

Fabiana imbricata (zones 8-10)
Mound-forming evergreen with needle-like,

x Fatshedera lizei

Hydrangea macrophylla 'Altona'

deep green leaves and tubular, mauve or white flowers in early summer. Height and spread 6 ft (1.8 m). The variety *F. i.* 'Prostrata' has pure white flowers. Height 36 in (90 cm), spread 6 ft (1.8 m).

x Fatshedera lizei (zones 7-10)
Spreading evergreen with large, shiny, leathery, dark green leaves and panicles of greenish-white flowers in autumn. Height 6 ft (1.8 m), spread 10 ft (3 m).

Fatsia japonica (zones 7-10)
Japanese aralia is a rounded evergreen shrub, spreading by suckers, with large, hand-like, dark green leaves and large umbels of creamy white flowers in autumn, followed by black fruit. Height and spread 10 ft (3 m).

Forsythia viridissima (zones 6-8)
Semi-evergreen (deciduous in cold areas), with mid-green leaves and bright, clear yellow flowers in early spring. Height and spread 5 ft (1.5 m).

Fothergilla gardenii (zones 5-9)
Bushy, deciduous shrub with dark green leaves that turn brilliant autumn colors of yellow, orange, red and purple. Small, white, fragrant flowers appear before the leaves in spring. Height and spread 4 ft (1.2 m).

Gaultheria
A genus of ericaceous evergreens, requiring acid soil conditions and particularly happy in a shady site.

Gaultheria forrestii (zones 7-8) is a spreading plant with glossy, dark green, bristly leaves and racemes of urn-shaped, fragrant white flowers in late spring and early summer followed by black fruit. Height 4 ft (1.2 m), spread 5 ft (1.5 m).

Gaultheria 'Shallon' (zones 6-8) is vigorous, spreading by suckers, with glossy mid-green leaves and urn-shaped, pink and white flowers in late spring and early summer, followed by purple fruit. Height and spread 4 ft (1.2 m).

Gaultheria x *wisleyensis* (zones 7-9) also spreads by suckers. It has small , dark green leaves and racemes of urn-shaped, white flowers in late spring and early summer, followed by deep red-purple fruit. Height and spread 36 in (90 cm).

Halimium lasianthum (zones 9-10)
Bushy, spreading evergreen with gray-green leaves and golden yellow flowers in spring and summer. Height 36 in (90 cm), spread 4 ft (1.2 m).

Hebe
Some other hebes are listed under **Low-growing Shrubs** (see page 139–40); as they are all evergreen even the taller varieties are excellent for ground cover.

Hebe brachysiphon 'White Gem' (zones 8-10) is compact with mid-green leaves and racemes of white flowers in summer. Height 30 in (75 cm), spread 36 in (90 cm).

Hebe x *franciscana* (zones 9-10) makes a rounded shrub with thick dark green leaves and light purple flowers in summer and autumn. Height and spread 36 in (90 cm). The variety *H.* x *f.* 'Variegata' has deep green leaves edged with creamy white.

Hebe 'Great Orme' (zones 9-10) is another rounded variety with purple shoots and shiny, mid-green leaves. Spikes of clear pink flowers fade to pale pink-white from summer through to late autumn. Height and spread 4 ft (1.2 m).

Helichrysum splendidum (zones 9-10)
Bushy evergreen with white woolly stems, silver-gray leaves and deep orange-yellow flowers in late summer and autumn. Height and spread 36 in (90 cm).

Hydrangea macrophylla 'Altona' (zones 6-9)
Deciduous shrub with glossy, dark green leaves and hortensia heads of rich pink or purple-blue flowers in mid- and late summer. Height 36 in (90 cm), spread 4 ft (1.2 m).

Hypericum
Not all hypericums are evergreen. I have included some semi-evergreens such as 'Rowallane' which may be deciduous if grown in a cold, exposed site, but which nevertheless make excellent ground cover when in leaf. *Hypericum* 'Eastleigh Gold'

Kolkwitzia amabilis

(zones 7-9) is a semi-evergreen with mid-green leaves and cup-shaped, bright yellow flowers in summer. Height and spread 4 ft (1.2 m). *H. kalmianum* (zones 5-7) is a bushy evergreen with blue-green leaves and saucer-shaped, golden yellow flowers in mid-summer. Height and spread 36 in (90 cm). *H.* 'Rowallane' (zones 7-9) has dark green leaves and large, golden yellow flowers in late summer and autumn. Height 6 ft (1.8 m), spread 36 in (90 cm).

Ilex crenata (zones 5-7)
Ilex crenata 'Bruns' is a low-growing evergreen holly with gray-green leaves good for ground cover, but is, unfortunately, a male form without fruit. Height 36 in (90 cm), spread 4 ft (1.2 m). The variety *I. c.* 'Golden Gem' is a compact low-form with deep yellow leaves turning pale yellow in summer and black berries. Height and spread 4 ft (1.2 m).

Itea yunnaniensis (zones 7-9)
Evergreen with spiny-toothed, dark green leaves and racemes of small white flowers in late summer and autumn. Height and spread 10 ft (3 m).

Jasminum
Jasminum fruticans (zones 8-10) is a bushy evergreen with dark green leaves and small fragrant, yellow flowers in summer. Height and spread 4 ft (1.2 m). *J. nudiflorum* (winter jasmine) (zones 6-9) is deciduous, with dark green leaves and bright yellow flowers appearing before the leaves in winter and early spring. Height and spread 10 ft (3 m).

Kalmia latifolia (zones 5-9)
Calico bush or mountain laurel is a bushy, evergreen with glossy, dark green leaves and large heads of cup-shaped, white, pale pink or dark pink flowers in late spring and early summer. The flowers open from tightly pinched deep pink or red buds, rather like cake decorations. Height and spread 10 ft (3 m).

Kolkwitzia amabilis (zones 5-9)
Beauty bush is a deciduous, suckering shrub

with dark green leaves that are often hidden in late spring and summer by a mass of deep pink flowers with cream throats. Height 10 ft (3 m), spread 13 ft (4 m).

Lavatera (zones 7-9)
Lavatera 'Barnsley' is a vigorous semi-evergreen with gray-green leaves and funnel-shaped, white flowers that turn dark pink with a red eye in summer. Height and spread 6 ft (1.8 m). *L.* 'Bressingham White' has saucer-shaped, pale pink flowers in summer and autumn. Height 6 ft (1.8 m), spread 5 ft (1.5 m).

Ledum groenlandicum (zones 2-6)
Labrador tea is a bushy evergreen with dark green leaves, pale brown felted on the underside. Terminal clusters of white flowers appear in late spring. Height 36 in (90 cm), spread 4 ft (1.2 m).

Leucothöe fontanesiana (zones 5-8)
Evergreen with leathery, glossy, dark green leaves and racemes of white flowers in spring. Height 6 ft (1.8 m), spread 10 ft (3 m). *L. f.* 'Rainbow' has dark green leaves with splashes of pink and cream. Height and spread 5 ft (1.5 m).

Leycesteria formosa (zones 8-10)
Himalayan honeysuckle is a thicket-forming, deciduous shrub with bamboo-like, bright green stems and dark green leaves. The pendant spikes of white flowers with deep purple bracts are followed by deep purple berries. Height and spread 6 ft (1.8 m).

Ligustrum delavayanum (zones 8-9)
Compact evergreen shrub with green leaves and panicles of white flowers in summer and early autumn, followed by blue-black fruit. Height 6 ft (1.8 m), spread 10 ft (3 m).

Lomatia tinctoria (zones 10-11)
Bushy, evergreen suckering shrub with dark green leaves and racemes of aromatic white flowers in summer. Height 36 in (90 cm), spread 4 ft (1.2 m).

Leucothoe fontanesiana 'Rainbow'

Lonicera
Members of this genus can be bushy shrubs or the more familiar climbing honeysuckles (some of which are listed under **Climbers**, page 95–96). During the first half of the twentieth century *Lonicera nitida* (zones 6-9) was used for garden hedging. It is fully evergreen and bushy with glossy, dark green leaves and small, creamy white flowers in spring, followed by purple berries. Height and spread 10 ft (3 m). The much smaller *L. n.* 'Baggesen's Gold' has bright gold leaves. Height and spread 4 ft (1.2 m).

Lonicera fragrantissima (zones 5-8) is a bushy, semi-evergreen shrub with dark green leaves blue-green on the underside and fragrant, creamy-white flowers produced at the leaf axils in winter and early spring. Height and spread 10 ft (3 m).

Lupinus arboreus (zones 8-9)
Tree lupin is a vigorous, evergreen with gray-green leaves and upright racemes of fragrant yellow flowers in late spring and summer. Height and spread 5 ft (1.5 m).

Mahonia

A large genus of evergreen shrubs; the lower-growing ones make excellent ground cover. *Mahonia japonica* 'Bealei' (zones 7-8) has sharp-toothed, blue-green leaves and upright racemes of fragrant yellow flowers in winter and early spring, followed by purple berries. Height 6 ft (1.8 m), spread 10 ft (3 m). *M. lomariifolia* (zones 8-9) is erect with long, shiny, sharp-toothed leaves and upright racemes of fragrant, clear yellow flowers in late autumn and winter. Height and spread 10 ft (3 m). *M. napaulensis* (zones 8-9) has glossy, dark green, sharp-toothed leaves and spreading racemes of clear yellow flowers in early spring, followed by white-coated, deep blue berries. Height and spread 10 ft (3 m).

Melicytus crassifolius (zones 9-10)

Twiggy, evergreen with leathery, dark green leaves and yellow flowers in spring and early summer, followed by purple berries. Height and spread 36 in (90 cm).

Myrtus communis (zones 8-9)

Common myrtle is an evergreen bushy shrub. Glossy, dark green leaves and white flowers with prominent tufts of white stamens in late summer and autumn are followed by purple-black berries. Height and spread 10 ft (3 m).

Nandina domestica (zones 6-9)

Heavenly bamboo is evergreen with mid-green leaves that are red-purple when young and again in winter. Panicles of star-shaped, white flowers with yellow anthers in summer are followed by bright red fruit. Height and spread 6 ft (1.8 m). The variety *N. d.* 'Harbor Dwarf' is similar, but grows to a height of only 36 in (90 cm) and spread of 4 ft (1.2 m).

Olearia

Olearia x *haastii* (zones 8-10) is a bushy evergreen with shiny, dark green leaves and daisy-like white flowers with yellow centers in late summer. Height 6 ft (1.8 m), spread 10 ft (3 m). *O. nummulariifolia* (zones 7-10)

is denser and the leaves are leathery and woolly-yellow on the underside. Fragrant, daisy-like white flowers with pale yellow centers appear during summer. Height and spread 6 ft (1.8 m).

Ozothamnus thyrsoideus (zones 9-10)

Evergreen with aromatic, dark green leaves and dense clusters of white flowers in summer. Height 10 ft (3 m), spread 6 ft (1.8 m).

Paeonia (zones 5-8)

Paeonia x *lemoinei* is a deciduous shrub, usually referred to as a tree peony, with dark green leaves and large, cup-shaped, white or yellow flowers with pink, orange or red marks in early summer. Height and spread 5 ft (1.5 m).

Another deciduous 'tree peony', *Paeonia suffruticosa*, has dark green leaves blue-green on the underside and large, single, white, pink or purple flowers in late spring and early summer. Height and spread 6 ft (1.8 m).

Philadelphus 'Belle Etoile' (zones 5-8)

Deciduous shrub with arching branches and mid-green leaves. The cup-shaped, single, fragrant flowers appear in late spring and early summer, with a pale purple blotch in the center of each bloom. Height 36 in (90 cm), spread 7 ft (2.2 m).

Phlomis fruticosa (zones 8-9)

Jerusalem sage is an evergreen shrub with wrinkled, gray-green leaves, woolly-green on the underside and deep yellow flowers in early summer. Height 36 in (90 cm), spread 5 ft (1.5 m).

Phygelius (zones 8-9)

Phygelius capensis (Cape figwort) is a suckering evergreen with dark green leaves. The upright panicles of orange flowers with red lobes and a yellow throat appear in summer. Height and spread 4 ft (1.2 m). *P.* x *rectus* has dark green leaves and pink-red flowers in summer. Height and spread 4 ft (1.2 m). The variety *P.* x. *r.* 'Moonraker' has pale cream flowers.

Pieris floribunda (zones 5-8)

Compact evergreen with glossy, dark green leaves and terminal panicles of white flowers in spring. Height 6 ft (1.8 m), spread 10 ft (3 m).

Pittosporum ralphii 'Wheeler's Dwarf' (zones 9-10)

Dense evergreen with shiny, deep green, wavy-edged leaves white felted on the underside and small, deep red flowers in spring. It is very slow-growing and hardy only in mild areas. Height 36 in (90 cm) spread 24 in (60 cm).

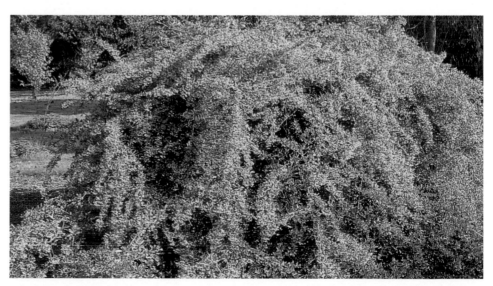

Left *Mahonia lonarifolia*

Pyracantha 'Golden Dome'

Vaccinium cylindraceum

Pseudowintera colorata (zones 9-10)
Bushy evergreen with leathery, pale green leaves marked pink and red and greenish yellow flowers in spring, followed by red berries that turn black. Height 36 in (90 cm), spread 5 ft (1.2 m).

Pyracantha (zones 6-9)
Pyracantha 'Golden Dome' is a spreading evergreen with glossy, bright green leaves and small white flowers in spring, followed by golden yellow berries. Height 6 ft (1.8 m), spread 10 ft (3 m). *P.* 'Santa Cruz' is lower, with dark green leaves. Small white flowers in early summer are followed by red berries. Height 36 in (90 cm), spread 7 ft (2.2 m).

Rhododendron
Rhododendron 'Britannia' (zones 7-9) is low-growing with pale green leaves and bell-shaped, bright red flowers in late spring and early summer. Height and spread 6 ft (1.8 m). The compact *R. ferrugineum* (Alpenrose) (zones 6-9) has glossy, dark green leaves, red-brown on the underside and deep pink to deep red flowers in early summer. Height and spread 4ft (1.2 m).
Rhododendron moupinense (zones 6-8) is a dwarf form with glossy dark green leaves pale

green on the underside and white, pink or deep pink flowers in late winter and early spring. Height and spread 4 ft (1.2 m). *R. yakushimanum* (zones 5-9) forms a dome shape with glossy, dark green leaves that are pale brown when young and red-brown on the underside and funnel-shaped, pale pink or white flowers in spring. Height and spread 6 ft (1.8 m).

Ribes laurifolium (zones 7-9)
Spreading evergreen with leathery, dark green leaves and pendant racemes of cup-shaped, greenish-yellow flowers in late winter and early spring, followed by red fruit, ripening to black on female flowers. Height 36 in (90 cm), spread 4 ft (1.2 m).

Ruscus aculeatus (zones 6-9)
Butcher's broom is an evergreen sub-shrub, spreading by suckers, with spine-tipped, glossy green cladophylls (instead of leaves) and bright red berries that are formed on the upper surface of the cladophylls on female plants Height 32 in (80 cm), spread 36 in (90 cm).

Ruta graveolens (zones 5-9)
Common rue is an evergreen with aromatic, blue-green leaves and dull yellow flowers in summer. Height 36 in (90 cm), spread 32 in (80 cm).

Skimmia x confusa 'Kew Green' (zones 6-9)
Compact evergreen with aromatic, gray-green leaves and panicles of fragrant, cream, male flowers in spring. Height and spread 5 ft (1.5 m).

Solanum laciniatum (zones 10-11)
Kangaroo apple is a vigorous evergreen with deep green leaves, purple shoots and dark blue flowers in summer and autumn, followed by orange fruit. Not fully hardy, it requires a frost-free site. Height and spread 6 ft (1.8 m).

Spiraea cantoniensis (zones 7-9)
Spreading semi-evergreen with deep, gray-green leaves and clusters of white flowers in early summer. Height 6 ft (1.8 m), spread 10 ft (3 m).

Ulex
Ulex europaeus 'Flore Pleno' (double gorse, whin or furze) (zones 6-8) is a dense, evergreen, spiny shrub with spine-like leaves and fragrant, bright yellow flowers produced intermittently throughout the year. Height and spread 6 ft (1.8 m). *U. gallii* (dwarf gorse) (zones 8-10) has pea-like bright yellow flowers in late summer and autumn. Height and spread 5 ft (1.5 m).

Vaccinium cylindraceum (zones 6-9)
Semi-evergreen with glossy dark green leaves and pendant racemes of purple-tinged green flowers in late summer and early autumn, followed by blue-black berries. Height and spread 7 ft (2.2 m).

Vestia foetida (zones 8-10)
Evergreen with shiny, dark green leaves that have an awful smell when crushed. Tubular, dull yellow flowers with protruding stamens are produced in spring and early summer. Height 7 ft (2.2 m), spread 5 ft (1.5 m).

Viburnum
I have chosen evergreen viburnums not only for their dense cover but because I love the variety of leaves, providing year-round interest. *V. davidii* (zones 8-9) is compact with shiny, dark green leaves and white flowers in late spring, followed by metallic-blue fruit. Both male and female plants are necessary if fruit is to be produced. Height and spread 4 ft (1.2 m). *V.* 'Pragense' (zones 6-8) is bushier with glossy, deep green leaves with deep veins and pink buds opening to white flowers in late spring. Height and spread 10 ft (3 m). *V. tinus* (laurustinus) (zones 8-10) has a similar height and spread, with dark green leaves. White flowers in winter and spring are followed by blue-black fruit.

Weigela
Weigela 'Eva Rathe' (zones 5-9) is a compact, deciduous shrub with dark green leaves and deep red buds opening to dark crimson flowers in late spring and early summer. Height and spread 5 ft (1.5 m). *W. middendorffiana* (zones 5-7) has mid-green leaves and bell-shaped, pale yellow flowers with red throat blotches in late spring and summer. Height and spread 4ft (1.2 m).

INDEX

Figures in **bold** refer to pages with illustrations

PHOTOGRAPHIC ACKNOWLEDGEMENTS

The publishers would especially like to thank

The Garden Picture Library
Unit 12, Ransome's Dock, 35 Parkgate Road
London, SW11 4NP
tel +44 (171) 228 4332   fax +44 (171) 924 3267

for their kind assistance in the production of this book

half-title Steven Wooster (Beth Chatto's garden); half-title verso Steven Wooster (Beth Chatto's garden); title page Heather Angel; pages 4–5 Rex Butcher/Garden Picture Library; pages 6–7 Steven Wooster (Ethridge Gardens, Timaru, New Zealand, design by Nan Raymond); page 8 Jacqui Hurst/GPL; page 9 Steven Wooster (Beth Chatto's garden); page 10 Brian Carter/GPL; page 11 John Glover/GPL; page 13 Philippe Bonduel/GPL; page 14 Heather Angel; page 17 top Andrea Jones; page 17 bottom Howard Rice/GPL; page 18 Steven Wooster (Beth Chatto's garden); page 19 both Jerry Harpur; page 21 Howard Rice/GPL; page 22 Marcus Harpur; page 25 John Glover/GPL; page 29 John Glover/GPL; page 32 Howard Rice/GPL; page 33 Christi Carter/GPL; page 34 Christopher Gallagher/GPL; page 35 Jerry Harpur; page 36 top John Cushnie; page 36 bottom Howard Rice/GPL; page 36/7 Steven Wooster/GPL; page 38 Steven Wooster (Beth Chatto's garden); page 39 top Juliette Wade/GPL; page 39 bottom Marcus Harpur; page 40 top Mayer/Le Scanff/GPL; page 40 bottom Steven Wooster (Beth Chatto's garden); page 41 Howard Rice/GPL; page 42 John Glover/GPL; page 43 both John Glover/GPL; page 44 Marcus Harpur; page 44/5 Jerry Harpur (Holker Hall); page 46 Sunniva Harte/GPL; page 47 top Brian Carter/GPL; page 47 bottom Didier Willery/GPL; page 48 John Glover/GPL; page 48/9 Tim Griffiths/GPL; page 49 bottom Neil Holmes/GPL; page 50 Didier Willery/ GPL; page 51 top John Cushnie; page 51 bottom Rex Butcher/GPL; page 52 Jacqui Hurst/GPL; page 53 top Steven Wooster (Beth Chatto's garden); page 53 bottom Howard Rice/GPL; page 54 top Neil Holmes/GPL; page 54 bottom Marcus Harpur; page 54/5 Steven Wooster (Beth Chatto's garden); page 56 Jacqui Hurst/GPL; page 57 Juliette Wade/GPL; page 58 top Sunniva Harte/GPL; page 58 bottom Marcus Harpur; page 58/9 Didier Willery/GPL; page 60 Neil Holmes/GPL; page 61 John Glover/GPL; page 62 top Brian Carter/GPL; page 62 bottom Rex Butcher/GPL; page 63 Jerry Harpur; page 64 Sunniva Harte/GPL; page 65 Sunniva Harte/GPL; page 66 top Joanne Pavia/GPL; page 66 bottom John Glover/GPL; page 67 Marcus Harpur; page 68 Rex Butcher/GPL; page 69 Mel Watson/GPL; page 70 both Neil Holmes/GPL; page 70/1 Philippe Bonduel/GPL; page 72 Brian Carter/GPL; page 73 Neil Holmes/GPL; page 74 top J S Sira/GPL; page 74 bottom left John Glover/GPL;

page 74 bottom right Lamontagne/GPL; page 75 Ron Evans/GPL; page 76 Didier Willery/GPL; page 77 Brian Carter/GPL; page 78 Howard Rice/GPL; page 79 Mark Bolton/GPL; page 80 Neil Holmes/GPL; page 81 Steven Wooster/GPL; page 82/3 John Miller/GPL; page 83 top Rex Butcher/ GPL; page 83 bottom Brian Carter/GPL; page 84 Clive Nichols/GPL; page 85 Geoff Dann/GPL; page 86 Heather Angel; page 86/7 Steven Wooster/GPL; page 88 Brigitte Thomas/GPL; page 89 J S Sira/GPL; page 90 Brian Carter/ GPL; page 90/91 Sunniva Harte/GPL; page 92 John Glover/GPL; page 93 J S Sira/GPL; page 94 JS Sira/GPL; page 95 J S Sira/GPL; page 96 John Glover/ GPL; page 97 top Didier Willery/GPL; page 97 bottom Jerry Pavia/GPL; page 98 top Heather Angel; page 98 bottom Brigittte Thomas/GPL; page 99 John Glover/GPL; page 100 top Marcus Harpur; page 100 bottom John Glover/GPL; page 101 Heather Angel; page 102 J S Sira/GPL; page 103 both John Glover/GPL; page 104 left Heather Angel; page 104/5 Marie O'Hara/GPL; page 105 right Sunniva Harte/GPL; page 106 left Jerry Pavia/GPL; page 106 right John Glover//GPL; page 107 Jerry Pavia/GPL; page 108 top Howard Rice/GPL; page 108 bottom John Glover/GPL; page 109 J S Sira/GPL; page 110 J S Sira/GPL; page 111 both Jerry Pavia/GPL; page 112 top Mayer/Le Scanff/GPL; page 112 bottom Christi CarterJ/GPL; page 113 Sunniva Harte/GPL; page 114 top Howard Rice/GPL; page 114 bottom Sunniva Harte/GPL (Beth Chatto's garden); page 115 Rex Butcher/GPL; page 116 Jerry Harpur (Beth Chatto's garden); page 117 Marcus Harpur; page 118 Ron Sutherland/GPL (Hackel Garden, Switzerland, Anthony Paul design); page 119 Lamontagne/GPL; page 120 John Glover/GPL; page 121 Marcus Harpur; page 122 John Glover/GPL; page 123 top Heather Angel; page 123 bottom Jerry Pavia/GPL; page 124 top Marcus Harpur; page 124 bottom Jerry Harpur; page 125 Heather Angel; page 126 Mayer/Le Scanff/GPL; page 127 top Ron Evans/GPL; page 127 bottom Howard Rice/GPL; page 128 Ron Sutherland/GPL (Godfrey Amy's garden, Jersey, Anthony Paul design); page 129 Jerry Pavia/GPL; page 130 both Jerry Pavia/GPL; page 131 top Howard Rice/GPL; page 131 bottom J S Sira/GPL; page 132 John Glover/GPL; page 133 top Neil Holmes/GPL; page 133 bottom Howard Rice/GPL; page 134 Howard Rice/GPL; page 135 Howard Rice/GPL; page 136 Jerry Pavia/GPL; page 137 top John Glover/GPL; page 137 bottom Neil Holmes/GPL; page 139 top Jerry Harpur (Beth Chatto's garden); page 139 bottom J S Sira/GPL; page 140 top John Glover/GPL; page 140 bottom Sunniva Harte/GPL; page 141 Jerry Pavia/GPL page 142; John Glover/GPL; page 143 Densey Clyne/GPL; page 144 John Glover/GPL; page 146 John Glover/GPL; page 147 top Jerry Pavia/GPL; page 147 right Steven Wooster/GPL; page 147 bottom Heather Angel; page 148 Howard Rice/GPL; page 149 Howard Rice/GPL; page 150 top John Glover/GPL; page 150 bottom Neil Holmes/GPL; page 151 Sunniva Harte/GPL; page 152 John Glover/GPL; page 153 John Glover/GPL; page 154 John Glover/GPL.